# ONE PAN
# DELICIOUS

*simple recipes from a single dish*

*from the*
HOFFMAN MEDIA TEST KITCHEN

# ONE PAN DELICIOUS

*simple recipes from a single dish*

83 Press
2323 2nd Avenue North
Birmingham, Alabama 35203
83press.com

ISBN 979-8-9923852-6-7
Printed in China

83 press®

# CONTENTS

# preface

On occasion, there are special meals worth pulling out every saucepan, skillet, and Dutch oven in your kitchen. For the day-to-day, the thought of making a meal with many steps (and many dishes to clean!) is overwhelming. Enter the one-pan recipe.

From heartwarming soups and cheesy pastas to roasted chicken and tasty pies, we've gathered our favorite one-pot recipes that simplify your cooking without sacrificing taste. Each dish overflows with flavor and will leave your friends and family with only one thing to say—delicious.

# EVERY DAY ESSENTIALS

Keep these items on hand to boost flavor and make weeknight cooking easier than ever.

## FLAVOR WITHOUT CHOPPING

Cut down on prep time with Air-Dried Shallots, Minced Garlic, and Minced Ginger in your recipes. These high-quality ingredients are peeled, minced, and freeze-dried at the peak of ripeness, making them an ideal solution for the busy home cook.

## FINISHING TOUCH

Good Flaked Sea Salt is a wonderful flavor and texture enhancer that's worth the splurge. If you want to be even more extravagant, look for Fleur de Sel.

## A TASTE OF FRANCE

Keep Herbes de Provence, a mixture of thyme, basil, savory, fennel, and lavender, in your spice drawer to instantly add layers of flavor to any recipe.

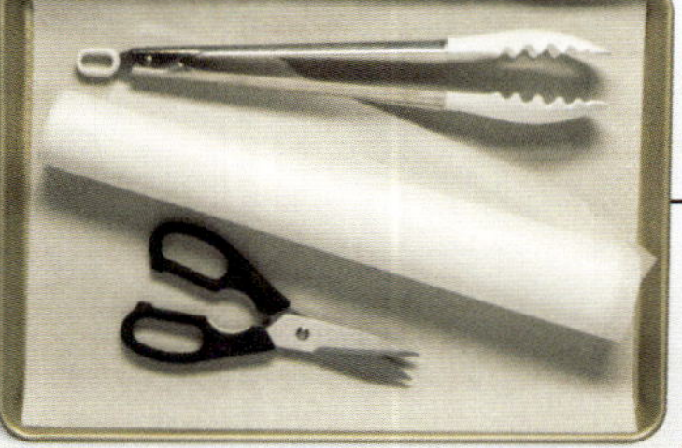

## **4 MUST-HAVE KITCHEN TOOLS** FOR EASY DINNER PREP

### TONGS

You can't have enough tongs. Use them for sautéing, searing, tossing, and serving.

### PARCHMENT PAPER

Line your pans with parchment to make cleanup even easier. Sure, foil works - but parchment is prettier.

### SHEET PANS

You can't roast vegetables and prepare dinner on one pan without this culinary workhorse.

### KITCHEN SHEARS

Your right hand in the kitchen! Use them to quickly cut herbs and meat.

Penzeys Minced
Garlic
Maldon
SEA SALT
FLAKES
CURIOUS CRYSTALS
LOVED BY CHEFS
THE WORLD OVER
Net Wt. 8.5oz 240g
100% NATURAL
HANDCRAFTED
FRANCE · AUX ANYSETIERS DU ROY · 45 BOULEVARD SAINT-GERMAIN 75005 PARIS
HERBES DE PROVENCE
POIDS NET 28g
HERBS OF PROVENCE
NET WEIGHT 1 oz
INGREDIENTS:
THYME, BASIL,
SAVORY, FENNEL SEEDS,
LAVENDER FLOWERS

# SOUPS, SALADS & SIDES

chapter 1

# BRAISED PORK POSOLE

**MAKES 8 SERVINGS**

*This take on the Mexican classic cooks mainly in the oven, creating deep flavor without having to stand watch over the stove.*

- **1 tablespoon ground cumin**
- **1 tablespoon dried Mexican oregano**
- **2 teaspoons kosher salt**
- **1 (4-pound) boneless pork shoulder, trimmed and cut into 8 pieces**
- **2 tablespoons olive oil, divided**
- **8 cups low-sodium chicken broth, divided**
- **8 chiles de árbol, stemmed**
- **1 large white onion, chopped**
- **6 cloves garlic, minced**
- **1 (14.5-ounce) can fire-roasted diced tomatoes**
- **1 bay leaf**
- **3 (15-ounce) cans white hominy, rinsed and drained**
- **Diced avocado, shredded cabbage, diced red onion, thinly sliced radish, and fresh cilantro, to serve**

**1.** Preheat oven to 350°.

**2.** In a small bowl, combine cumin, oregano, and salt. Rub spice mixture all over pork. In a large enamel-coated cast-iron Dutch oven, heat 1 tablespoon oil over medium heat. Add pork in batches; cook until browned on all sides. Add 1 cup broth; cover with lid.

**3.** Bake for 2 hours. Drain cooking liquid through a fat separator, and reserve. Shred meat, and reserve in a large bowl. Wipe Dutch oven clean.

**4.** To same Dutch oven, add chiles; cook over medium heat until puffed. Transfer chiles to the container of a blender; add 2 cups broth, and process until smooth. Set aside.

**5.** To same Dutch oven, heat remaining 1 tablespoon oil over medium-high heat. Add onion and garlic; cook, stirring frequently, until slightly tender, about 5 minutes. Add pork and reserved cooking liquid, puréed chile mixture, tomatoes, bay leaf, and remaining 5 cups broth; cook for 45 minutes.

**6.** Add hominy, and cook for 15 minutes. Serve with avocado, cabbage, onion, radish, and cilantro.

# SPRING PEA SOUP

**MAKES 4 TO 6 SERVINGS**

*A swirl of sour cream and a sprinkle of fresh dill make this soup look more like a work of art than a light lunch.*

**2 tablespoons unsalted butter**
**1 medium yellow onion, chopped**
**4 cloves garlic, minced**
**4 cups low-sodium chicken broth**
**1 small russet potato, peeled and chopped**
**2 pounds fresh or thawed frozen green peas**
**2½ teaspoons kosher salt**
**¼ teaspoon ground black pepper**
**Sour cream, fresh dill, and ground black pepper, to serve**

**1.** In a medium Dutch oven, melt butter over medium-high heat. Add onion and garlic; cook until just tender, about 5 minutes. Add broth and potato; bring to a boil. Reduce heat to medium-low; simmer until potatoes are tender, about 15 minutes. Add peas, salt, and pepper; cook for 1 minute. Remove from heat.

**2.** Working in batches, transfer soup to the container of a blender; purée until smooth. Serve with sour cream, dill, and pepper.

# FRENCH ONION SOUP

**MAKES 8 TO 10 SERVINGS**

*Crumbled bacon adds a smoky flavor to this indulgent soup that'll transport you to a bistro in France.*

- ½ pound thick-cut bacon, chopped
- 1 cup unsalted butter
- 3 pounds yellow onions, sliced
- 4 cloves garlic, smashed
- 4 bay leaves
- 4 sprigs fresh thyme
- 2 teaspoons kosher salt
- 1 teaspoon ground black pepper
- 1 cup sherry
- ¼ cup all-purpose flour
- 2 (32-ounce) cartons beef broth
- 1 French baguette, sliced ½ inch thick
- 3 cups shredded Gruyère cheese

**1.** In a 4- to 6-quart cast-iron Dutch oven, cook bacon over medium heat until crisp. Remove bacon using a slotted spoon, and let drain on paper towels, reserving drippings in pot.

**2.** Melt butter with drippings in pot. Add onion, garlic, bay leaves, thyme, salt, and pepper; cook, stirring frequently, until onions are very soft and caramelized, about 35 minutes.

**3.** Add sherry, and bring to a boil. Reduce heat, and simmer until sherry has evaporated, about 6 minutes. Discard bay leaves and thyme. Reduce heat to low; sprinkle flour onto onion mixture. Cook, stirring constantly, for 5 minutes. Stir in broth; cook over medium heat for 15 minutes.

**4.** Preheat oven to 350°. Line a large rimmed baking sheet with foil. Arrange bread slices on prepared pan.

**5.** Bake until bread is completely dry, about 10 minutes. Remove from oven; preheat oven to broil.

**6.** Divide soup among 8 to 10 broiler-proof serving bowls. Place bowls on baking sheet. Top each with 2 bread slices and ½ cup cheese.

**7.** Broil until cheese is melted and bubbly, about 2 minutes. Sprinkle with bacon. Serve immediately.

# APPLE AND BEER CHEESE SOUP

**MAKES 6 SERVINGS**

*This cozy soup has complex flavor thanks to tart apple, sweet onion, and IPA beer.*

- **5 tablespoons salted butter, divided**
- **1 cup chopped sweet onion**
- **½ cup chopped carrot**
- **1½ cups chopped peeled Granny Smith apple**
- **½ teaspoon kosher salt**
- **½ teaspoon ground black pepper**
- **¼ teaspoon dry mustard**
- **¼ teaspoon ground red pepper**
- **1 clove garlic, minced**
- **¼ cup all-purpose flour**
- **1 (12-ounce) bottle IPA beer**
- **1 cup chicken stock**
- **1 cup whole milk**
- **6 ounces shredded sharp Cheddar cheese**
- **4 ounces shredded smoked Gouda cheese**
- **1 cup cubed marbled rye bread**
- **½ cup chopped pecans, toasted**

**1.** In a large Dutch oven, melt 3 tablespoons butter over medium heat. Add onion, carrot, apple, salt, and black pepper; cook until mixture becomes tender, about 5 minutes. Add dry mustard, red pepper, and garlic; cook, stirring often, until mixture is tender, about 3 minutes. Add flour; cook, stirring constantly, for 3 minutes.

**2.** Reduce heat to medium-low and slowly add beer, stock, and milk, stirring constantly. Increase heat to medium-high and boil, stirring constantly, until thickened, about 3 minutes. Remove from heat; let stand for 3 minutes. Working in batches, process mixture in a blender until very smooth. Return mixture to Dutch oven and heat over medium-low heat. Working in batches, add cheeses, stirring until cheese melts.

**3.** In a small skillet, melt remaining 2 tablespoons butter over medium-high heat. Add bread, stirring constantly, until toasted, about 5 minutes. Top each serving with croutons and pecans.

# CHICKEN AND RICE SOUP

**MAKES ABOUT 6 SERVINGS**

*A bowl of this cozy chicken soup makes for a deliciously hearty dinner.*

- **2 tablespoons unsalted butter**
- **1 tablespoon canola oil**
- **1½ cups chopped yellow onion**
- **½ cup chopped celery**
- **1½ cups wild rice blend***
- **2 large cloves garlic, minced**
- **7 cups chicken broth, divided**
- **1½ cups coarsely chopped carrot**
- **1 (8-ounce) package fresh baby portobello mushrooms, quartered**
- **2 tablespoons chopped fresh thyme**
- **2 tablespoons chopped fresh parsley**
- **2½ teaspoons kosher salt, divided**
- **½ teaspoon ground black pepper**
- **5 cups shredded cooked chicken**
- **⅔ cup heavy whipping cream**
- **Garnish: chopped fresh parsley, chopped fresh thyme**

**1.** In a medium Dutch oven, heat butter and oil over medium-high heat until butter is melted. Add onion and celery; cook until softened, about 4 minutes. Stir in rice and garlic; cook for 2 minutes, stirring frequently. Stir in 6 cups broth, carrot, mushrooms, thyme, parsley, 2 teaspoons salt, and pepper; bring to a boil. Partially cover; reduce heat, and simmer until rice is almost tender, about 35 minutes. Stir in chicken, cream, remaining 1 cup broth, and remaining ½ teaspoon salt; cook until rice is tender, about 10 minutes. Garnish with parsley and thyme, if desired.

**We used Lundberg Wild Blend Rice.*

# TEXAS-STYLE CHILI

**MAKES ABOUT 3 QUARTS**

*Texans debate whether their style of chili should have tomatoes or if the beef should be ground or in pieces, but the one unifying rule is absolutely no beans allowed.*

- 2 tablespoons vegetable oil, plus more as needed
- 4 pounds beef chuck roast, trimmed and cut into 1-inch pieces
- 1 tablespoon ground cumin
- 2 teaspoons ground coriander
- 2 teaspoons ancho chile powder
- 1 tablespoon kosher salt
- 1 teaspoon ground black pepper
- 2 cups chopped yellow onion
- 1 cup diced seeded assorted chile peppers
- ¼ cup minced garlic
- 1 tablespoon dried oregano
- 2 tablespoons masa harina
- 2 (12-ounce) bottles or cans dark lager beer*
- 1 cup water
- 1 tablespoon puréed canned chipotles in adobo sauce
- Sliced red onion, sliced fresh jalapeño, halved cherry tomatoes, shredded cheese, fresh cilantro, flour tortillas, and lime wedges, to serve

**1.** In a 4- to 6-quart cast-iron Dutch oven, heat oil over medium-high heat.

**2.** In a large bowl, stir together beef, cumin, coriander, ancho chile powder, salt, and black pepper until well combined. Working in 3 to 4 batches, cook beef pieces until browned all over, 1 to 2 minutes per side, adding more oil as needed between batches. Transfer all beef to a bowl.

**3.** Add onion, chile peppers, garlic, and oregano to pot. Cook over medium heat, stirring occasionally, until softened, 3 to 5 minutes. Stir in masa harina. Stir in beer, 1 cup water, puréed chipotles, and beef; bring to a boil over medium-high heat, stirring occasionally. Reduce heat to medium-low; cover and cook, stirring occasionally, until beef is tender, about 1 hour.

**4.** Uncover and cook, stirring occasionally, until beef is very tender and liquid is slightly thickened and reduced, 20 to 30 minutes. Serve with desired toppings.

**We used Negra Modelo.*

# BROWN RICE SALAD

**MAKES 8 TO 10 SERVINGS**

*This salad is delicious served warm, at room temperature, or chilled, making it a great choice for meal prepping or taking to any gathering.*

- **2 cups water**
- **1 cup brown rice***
- **1 teaspoon kosher salt, divided**
- **1 large Honeycrisp apple, cored and sliced ¼ inch thick**
- **1 (15.5-ounce) can black-eyed peas, rinsed and drained**
- **4 cups baby spinach**
- **½ cup dried cranberries**
- **½ cup chopped toasted walnuts**
- **¼ cup chopped green onion**
- **3 tablespoons fresh lemon juice**
- **1½ tablespoons country-style Dijon mustard**
- **¾ teaspoon garlic powder**
- **¾ teaspoon ground black pepper**
- **6 tablespoons olive oil**
- **Garnish: chopped green onion, chopped walnuts**

**1.** Line a large rimmed baking sheet with parchment paper.
**2.** In a medium saucepan, bring 2 cups water, rice, and ¼ teaspoon salt to a boil over medium-high heat. Cover, reduce heat to medium-low, and cook until tender, about 20 minutes. Remove from heat, and let sit, covered, for 5 minutes. Fluff with a fork; place in an even layer on prepared pan. Let cool at room temperature for 15 minutes.
**3.** In a large bowl, toss together cooled rice, apple, black-eyed peas, spinach, cranberries, walnuts, and green onion.
**4.** In a small bowl, whisk together lemon juice, mustard, garlic powder, pepper, and remaining ¾ teaspoon salt. Gradually whisk in oil until smooth. Add ½ cup dressing to salad, tossing to coat. Garnish with green onion and walnuts, if desired. Serve with remaining ¼ cup dressing.

**We used Anson Mills Charleston Gold Brown Rice.*

# WILTED SAAG PANEER SALAD

MAKES 4 SERVINGS

*Use a sturdier leaf spinach such as Bloomsdale for this recipe. If you only have baby spinach available, drizzle the hot oil over the leaves in a large bowl and toss until coated instead of tossing the leaves in the skillet. This will keep the leaves from wilting too much.*

**½ cup chopped red onion**
**6 tablespoons olive oil, divided**
**10 to 12 ounces fresh paneer cheese, cubed**
**Kosher salt, to taste**
**1 jalapeño, seeded and finely chopped**
**2 cloves garlic, minced**
**2 teaspoons minced fresh ginger**
**1¼ teaspoons garam masala**
**Ground black pepper, to taste**
**¾ pound Bloomsdale spinach, torn**
**1½ tablespoons fresh lemon juice**
**1 cup halved cherry tomatoes**

**1.** Soak onion in cold water for 15 minutes. Drain.
**2.** In a large heavy-bottomed skillet, heat 2 tablespoons oil over medium heat until hot. Add jalapeño, garlic, and ginger; sauté until lightly golden, 1 to 2 minutes. Add garam masala, and cook for 1 minute, stirring constantly.
**3.** Season cheese with salt. Add cheese in three batches to sauté, turning frequently, until golden on all sides, 4 to 5 minutes. Remove cheese using a slotted spoon, and let drain on paper towels. Wipe skillet clean.
**4.** Add remaining 4 tablespoons oil to skillet, and heat over medium heat. Season oil with salt and black pepper. Fold in spinach, a handful at a time, and cook, turning leaves constantly, until spinach is starting to slightly wilt, 30 seconds to 1 minute. Transfer to a serving bowl, and toss with lemon juice. Fold in onion, cheese, and tomatoes. Season with salt and black pepper. Serve immediately.

# BLACK-EYED PEA SALAD WITH SMOKY SORGHUM DRESSING

**MAKES 4 TO 6 SERVINGS**

*Fresh, sweet, and smoky, this lovely salad has it all.*

**SALAD**

- 1 cup dried black-eyed peas*
- 4 cups low-sodium vegetable stock
- 1 teaspoon kosher salt
- 1 cup fresh corn kernels (about 2 ears)
- 1 cup quartered cherry tomatoes
- ½ cup chopped red bell pepper
- 1 cup chopped celery
- ½ cup chopped red onion
- ¼ cup chopped fresh parsley
- ½ cup bacon, cooked and crumbled (5 to 6 slices)

**SMOKY SORGHUM DRESSING**

- ¼ cup apple cider vinegar
- 2 tablespoons sorghum syrup
- 1 clove garlic, minced
- 1 tablespoon smoked paprika
- ½ teaspoon kosher salt
- ¼ teaspoon ground black pepper
- ½ cup vegetable oil

**FOR SALAD**

**1.** Rinse and sort peas, and place in a large bowl. Add water to cover by 2 inches. Cover bowl, and let stand overnight. Drain peas.

**2.** In a 3-quart saucepan, add peas, vegetable stock, and salt; bring to a boil over medium-high heat. Reduce heat to medium-low, and simmer until peas are tender, about 2 hours. Drain and rinse with cold water. Chill until ready to use.

**3.** In a medium bowl, combine cooked peas, corn, tomatoes, bell pepper, celery, and onion. Toss with desired amount of Smoky Sorghum Dressing, and chill for at least 1 hour. Just before serving, stir in parsley and bacon.

**FOR DRESSING**

**1.** In a medium bowl, mix together vinegar, sorghum, garlic, paprika, salt, and black pepper. Slowly whisk in oil.

**We used Camellia Brand Black-eyed Peas.*

# INDIAN-SPICED OKRA

MAKES ABOUT 4 TO 6 SERVINGS

*Toasted mustard seeds and other bold spices, like coriander and curry powder, take this okra to a whole new level.*

- **1 teaspoon mustard seeds**
- **1 pound fresh okra, trimmed**
- **1 small Fresno pepper, seeded and cut into ⅛-inch-thick slices**
- **1 tablespoon olive oil**
- **1¼ teaspoons kosher salt**
- **1 teaspoon ground coriander**
- **½ teaspoon ground black pepper**
- **¼ teaspoon curry powder**

**Garnish: chopped fresh parsley**

**1.** Heat a large skillet over medium-high heat. Add mustard seeds; cook, stirring occasionally, until toasted, about 30 seconds. Add okra, Fresno pepper, oil, salt, coriander, black pepper, and curry powder; cook for 1 minute, stirring frequently.

**2.** Reduce heat to medium-low; cover and cook for 8 minutes, stirring occasionally. Increase heat to medium-high; uncover and cook until okra is lightly browned and tender, about 2 minutes more. Garnish with parsley, if desired.

# SCALLOPED POTATO, PARSNIP, TURNIP, AND FENNEL CASSEROLE

MAKES 6 TO 8 SERVINGS

*Thinly sliced root vegetables smothered in heavy cream, cheese, and herbs make for a can't-resist side dish.*

- **4 tablespoons unsalted butter, softened and divided**
- **2½ cups (¼-inch-thick) sliced peeled Yukon gold potatoes (about 3 large)**
- **2½ cups (¼-inch-thick) sliced parsnips (about 5 medium)**
- **2½ cups (¼-inch-thick) sliced peeled turnips (about 3 large)**
- **2 cups (¼-inch-thick) sliced fennel (about 1 medium)**
- **¾ cup shredded Parmesan cheese, divided**
- **2 cups heavy whipping cream**
- **1 cup chicken stock**
- **2 tablespoons chopped fresh thyme**
- **1 teaspoon kosher salt**
- **½ teaspoon ground black pepper**
- **Garnish: fresh thyme, fennel fronds**

**1.** Preheat oven to 400°. Spread 1 tablespoon softened butter in bottom and up sides of a 12-inch enamel-coated cast-iron braiser.
**2.** In a large bowl, toss together potatoes, parsnips, turnips, fennel, and ½ cup cheese. Layer vegetables in prepared pan.
**3.** In a small saucepan, heat cream, stock, thyme, salt, pepper, and remaining 3 tablespoons butter over medium heat, stirring occasionally, until butter is melted and bubbles begin to form around sides of pan (do not fully boil). Pour mixture over vegetables.
**4.** Bake for 30 minutes. Sprinkle remaining ¼ cup cheese onto vegetables. Bake until vegetables are tender and golden brown, about 15 minutes more. Let stand for 15 minutes before serving. Garnish with thyme and fennel fronds, if desired.

# ROASTED GREEN BEANS

MAKES 6 TO 8 SERVINGS

*We swapped the baking dish for a sheet pan to make a side dish full of classic flavor.*

- **2 pounds fresh green beans, trimmed**
- **1 large red onion, sliced (about ¾ pound)**
- **1 (8-ounce) package sliced fresh baby portobello mushrooms**
- **4 slices center-cut bacon, chopped**
- **¼ cup canola oil**
- **2¼ teaspoons kosher salt**
- **¾ teaspoon ground black pepper**
- **1 tablespoon chopped fresh thyme**
- **1 tablespoon apple cider vinegar**
- **1 cup crumbled pork rinds**

**1.** Preheat oven to 425°. Line a large baking sheet with parchment paper.

**2.** Spread beans, onion, mushrooms, and bacon on prepared pan so they fit in a single layer. (Use two baking sheets, if necessary.) Drizzle with oil, and sprinkle with salt and pepper, tossing to coat.

**3.** Roast until vegetables are browned and tender, 30 to 35 minutes. Toss with thyme and vinegar. Top with pork rinds. Serve immediately.

# ROASTED VEGETABLES WITH CREAMY HERB DRESSING

MAKES 6 TO 8 SERVINGS

*A simple mix of roasted vegetables is hard to beat, and a drizzle of creamy lemon dressing amps up the flavor.*

### ROASTED VEGETABLES

- ½ pound asparagus, cut diagonally into 2-inch pieces
- ½ pound Brussels sprouts, trimmed and halved lengthwise
- ½ pound multicolored carrots, peeled and cut diagonally into ½-inch pieces
- ½ red onion, halved lengthwise and cut into wedges
- 3 tablespoons olive oil
- 1 teaspoon kosher salt
- ½ teaspoon ground black pepper

### CREAMY HERB DRESSING

- ½ cup mayonnaise
- 1 clove garlic, minced
- 1 teaspoon lemon zest
- 2 tablespoons fresh lemon juice
- 2 tablespoons minced fresh rosemary
- 1 tablespoon water
- 1 tablespoon whole-grain mustard
- 1½ teaspoons light brown sugar
- 1 teaspoon hot sauce
- ½ teaspoon kosher salt

### FOR VEGETABLES

**1.** Preheat oven to 375°.

**2.** In a large bowl, toss together asparagus, Brussels sprouts, carrot, onion, olive oil, salt, and pepper, tossing to coat. Spread vegetables in a single layer on a 14-inch cast-iron baking pan.

**3.** Bake until vegetables are tender, 30 to 35 minutes. Serve with Creamy Herb Dressing.

### FOR DRESSING

**1.** In a medium bowl, whisk together all ingredients until well combined. Cover and refrigerate for up to 2 weeks.

# COWBOY BAKED BEANS

**MAKES 8 SERVINGS**

*Hearty and full of flavor, you can't beat these souped-up beans.*

- **1 cup barbecue sauce**
- **⅓ cup sorghum syrup**
- **1 teaspoon ground cumin**
- **1 teaspoon chili powder**
- **1 teaspoon smoked paprika**
- **¼ teaspoon ground red pepper**
- **2 (15.5-ounce) cans kidney beans, drained and rinsed**
- **1 (28-ounce) can baked beans**
- **1 (16-ounce) package thick-cut bacon**
- **1 pound lean ground beef**
- **1 tablespoon vegetable oil**
- **½ cup chopped yellow onion**
- **½ cup chopped red bell pepper**
- **½ cup chopped green bell pepper**

**1.** Preheat oven to 350°.
**2.** In a medium bowl, mix together barbecue sauce, sorghum, cumin, chili powder, paprika, red pepper, and beans.
**3.** In a 12-inch cast-iron skillet, cook bacon over medium heat until soft but cooked through, 4 to 5 minutes; remove, reserving 1 tablespoon drippings in pan, and let drain on paper towels.
**4.** In same skillet, add beef, and cook over medium heat, stirring occasionally, until browned. Remove beef, and drain. Wipe skillet clean.
**5.** In same skillet, heat oil over medium-high heat. Add onion and red and green bell peppers, and cook until tender and onions turn golden brown, 5 to 6 minutes. Stir in ground beef and bean mixture. Place bacon on top of beans.
**6.** Bake until bacon is golden brown and beans are bubbly, 30 to 35 minutes.

# ASPARAGUS WITH MINT AND LEMON VINAIGRETTE

MAKES 3 TO 4 SERVINGS

*While a drizzle of lemon vinaigrette and a dusting of fresh mint is all this seasonal produce needs to become a showstopper, salted pistachios add nice texture and crunch, perfectly rounding out this simple side.*

- **1 teaspoon lemon zest, plus more for garnish**
- **3 tablespoons fresh lemon juice**
- **⅓ teaspoon kosher salt, divided**
- **⅓ teaspoon ground black pepper, divided**
- **8 tablespoons olive oil, divided**
- **4 tablespoons chopped fresh mint, divided**
- **1 pound fresh, thick-stemmed asparagus, trimmed and halved lengthwise**
- **2 tablespoons chopped roasted salted pistachios**

**Garnish: chopped fresh mint, chopped roasted salted pistachios**

**1.** In a small bowl, whisk together lemon zest and juice, ¼ teaspoon kosher salt, and ¼ teaspoon ground black pepper. Whisk in 6 tablespoons olive oil and 2 tablespoons mint.

**2.** In a large skillet, heat remaining 2 tablespoons olive oil over medium-high heat. Add asparagus; cook, turning occasionally, until browned and tender, 6 to 8 minutes. Sprinkle with reamaining ¼ teaspoon kosher salt and remaining ¼ teaspoon ground black pepper.

**3.** Transfer asparagus to a serving platter. Drizzle with ¼ cup lemon mixture. Sprinkle with pistachios and remaining 2 tablespoons mint. Garnish with additional mint and pistachios, if desired.

# SORGHUM-GLAZED ROASTED VEGETABLES

MAKES 8 SERVINGS

*Your side dish plans are set thanks to this tasty roasted recipe.*

- ⅓ cup sorghum syrup
- 3 tablespoons orange zest
- 3 tablespoons unsalted butter, melted
- 1 clove garlic, minced
- 2 tablespoons apple cider vinegar
- 2 tablespoons whole-grain mustard
- ¼ teaspoon crushed red pepper
- 1 pound rainbow carrots, peeled, cut in half lengthwise
- 1 pound parsnips, peeled and cut into fourths lengthwise
- 1 large onion, cut into ⅛-inch slices
- ½ pound beets, peeled, cut in half, or quartered if large
- Garnish: fresh sage, flaked sea salt

**1.** Preheat oven to 400°. Line a rimmed baking sheet with foil and lightly grease with cooking spray.
**2.** In a small bowl, mix together sorghum, orange zest, butter, garlic, vinegar, mustard, and red pepper until combined.
**3.** In a large bowl, add carrot, parsnip, and onion, and toss with three-fourths of the dressing. Place on prepared baking sheet.
**4.** On a 6x6-inch square of foil, add beet and top with remaining dressing. Pull sides of foil around beet but do not seal. Place on prepared baking sheet.
**5.** Bake until vegetables are tender, 30 to 40 minutes, stirring halfway through baking. Place vegetables on serving platter. Garnish with sage and flaky sea salt, if desired. Serve immediately.

# MELTING SWEET POTATOES

MAKES 6 TO 8 SERVINGS

*With a beautiful crisp crust and a super soft interior, this dish takes the humble sweet potato to new heights.*

- **2 tablespoons vegetable oil**
- **4 medium sweet potatoes, peeled and cut into 1-inch slices**
- **1 cup beef broth**
- **2 tablespoons minced shallot**
- **2 cloves garlic, minced**
- **¾ cup unsalted butter, cubed**
- **1 tablespoon Cajun seasoning***
- **2 sprigs fresh thyme**
- **2 sprigs fresh rosemary**

**1.** Preheat oven to 400°.
**2.** In a 12-inch cast-iron skillet, heat oil over medium-high heat. Place sweet potato slices in a single layer in oil. Cook until browned, 3 to 4 minutes per side.
**3.** In a small bowl, stir together broth, shallot, and garlic, and pour over sweet potatoes. Sprinkle butter and Cajun seasoning on top. Top with thyme and rosemary.
**4.** Bake until tender, about 30 minutes.

**We used Slap Ya Mama Original Blend Cajun Seasoning.*

# CHEESY ASPARAGUS WITH SMOKED ALMONDS

MAKES 6 TO 8 SERVINGS

*A mix of Parmesan, smoked Gouda, and smoked almonds adds a flavorful flare to this classic vegetable.*

- 2 pounds fresh asparagus, trimmed
- 2 tablespoons olive oil
- 1 tablespoon sherry vinegar
- 2 shallots, thinly sliced
- 2 cloves garlic, minced
- 1 teaspoon Dijon mustard
- ½ teaspoon kosher salt
- ½ teaspoon ground black pepper
- ½ cup shredded Parmesan cheese, divided
- ½ cup shredded smoked Gouda cheese, divided
- ⅓ cup chopped smoked almonds

**1.** Preheat oven to 375°.

**2.** In a large bowl, toss together asparagus, oil, vinegar, shallots, garlic, mustard, salt, and pepper until well coated. Spread half of asparagus mixture onto a large cast-iron griddle. Sprinkle with ¼ cup Parmesan and ¼ cup Gouda. Spread remaining half of asparagus mixture onto cheeses; sprinkle with remaining ¼ cup Parmesan and remaining ¼ cup Gouda.

**3.** Bake until asparagus is tender and cheeses are bubbly and beginning to brown, 15 to 20 minutes. Top with almonds. Serve immediately.

# BREADS

# chapter 2

# BACON CHEDDAR JALAPEÑO MONKEY BREAD

**MAKES 8 SERVINGS**

*Add a little heat to your bread basket with these spicy and cheesy pull-apart rolls.*

- **1 cup warm whole milk (105° to 110°), divided**
- **1 (0.25-ounce) package active dry yeast**
- **⅓ cup plus ½ cup unsalted butter, melted and divided**
- **¼ cup sugar**
- **¼ cup sour cream**
- **1 large egg**
- **3½ to 4 cups all-purpose flour, divided**
- **1¾ teaspoons kosher salt, divided**
- **1 (8-ounce) block sharp Cheddar cheese, shredded**
- **1½ teaspoons garlic powder**
- **½ teaspoon Italian seasoning**
- **1 pound bacon, cooked and roughly chopped**
- **1½ jalapeños, seeded and thinly sliced**

**1.** In a medium bowl, combine ¾ cup warm milk and yeast. Let stand until mixture is foamy, about 10 minutes.

**2.** In the bowl of a stand mixer fitted with the paddle attachment, stir together ⅓ cup melted butter, sugar, sour cream, egg, and remaining ¼ cup warm milk.

**3.** In a large bowl, whisk together 3½ cups flour and 1¼ teaspoons salt. Add half of flour mixture to butter mixture. With mixer on low speed, add yeast mixture, beating just until combined. Beat in remaining flour mixture. Switch to the dough hook attachment. Beat at medium speed until dough is smooth and elastic, about 3 minutes, adding remaining ½ cup flour if needed. (Dough should not be sticky.)

**4.** Spray a large bowl with cooking spray. Place dough in bowl, turning to grease top. Loosely cover and let rise in a warm, draft-free place (75°) until doubled in size, about 1 hour.

**5.** Line a 10-inch cast-iron skillet with parchment paper.

**6.** Gently punch down dough, and divide into 32 dough balls.

**7.** In a medium bowl, stir together Cheddar, garlic powder, remaining ½ teaspoon salt, and Italian seasoning. Coat 16 dough balls in remaining ½ cup melted butter, and roll in cheese mixture. Reserve remaining cheese mixture. Place coated dough balls in prepared skillet, layering with three-fourths of bacon and three-fourths of jalapeño. Coat remaining dough balls in melted butter, and place on top. Drizzle with remaining melted butter.

**8.** Cover and let rise in a warm, draft-free place (75°) until puffed, about 20 minutes.

**9.** Preheat oven to 350°. Bake, covered in foil, until a wooden pick inserted in center comes out clean, about 55 minutes. Uncover and sprinkle with remaining cheese mixture, remaining bacon, and remaining jalapeño. Bake until cheese is melted, about 5 minutes more. Let cool for 10 minutes before serving.

# DUTCH OVEN SUPREME PIZZA

**MAKES 1 (12- TO 14-INCH) PIZZA**

*Don't have time to make homemade dough? Buy a 16-ounce bag of pizza dough from the grocery store deli to use instead.*

**DOUGH**

- 1⅓ cups warm water (105° to 110°)
- 1 teaspoon sugar
- 1 (0.25-ounce) package active dry yeast
- 3¼ cups all-purpose flour, divided
- 2 tablespoons plain yellow cornmeal
- 1 tablespoon plus 2 teaspoons extra-virgin olive oil, divided
- 2 teaspoons kosher salt
- 1 tablespoon olive oil

**PIZZA**

- ½ cup pizza sauce
- 1 cup shredded mozzarella cheese, divided
- 1 cup crumbled cooked Italian sausage
- ½ cup thinly sliced yellow onion
- ½ cup chopped green bell pepper
- ¼ cup pepperoni slices
- ¼ cup sliced black olives
- ¼ cup grated Parmesan cheese
- 1 teaspoon chopped fresh oregano
- ¼ teaspoon ground black pepper

Garnish: chopped fresh basil

## FOR DOUGH

**1.** In the bowl of a stand mixer fitted with the dough hook attachment, stir together 1⅓ cups warm water, sugar, and yeast by hand. Let stand until mixture is foamy, about 5 minutes. Add 2 cups flour, cornmeal, 1 tablespoon oil, and salt, and beat at medium speed for 2 minutes. Add 1 cup flour, and beat until a soft, sticky dough forms. Continue beating until dough pulls away from sides of bowl.

**2.** Turn out dough onto a lightly floured surface, and knead until smooth and elastic, 5 to 6 minutes, using remaining ¼ cup flour as needed to keep dough from sticking to hands, if necessary. Lightly brush a large bowl with remaining 2 teaspoons oil. Place dough in bowl, turning to grease top. Cover and let rise in a warm, draft-free place (75°) until doubled in size, about 1 hour and 15 minutes.

**3.** Preheat oven to 450°. Place a 6-quart enameled cast-iron Dutch oven or 12-inch braiser in bottom third of oven to preheat.

**4.** Lightly punch down dough. Turn out dough onto a lightly floured surface; cover and let stand for 5 minutes. Roll dough into a 12-inch circle. Fold dough over a rolling pin, and carefully place on a piece of parchment paper. Brush dough with oil.

## FOR PIZZA

**1.** Spread pizza sauce onto dough, leaving a ¼-inch border. Sprinkle with ½ cup mozzarella. Top with sausage, onion, bell pepper, pepperoni, olives, Parmesan, and remaining ½ cup mozzarella. Sprinkle with oregano and black pepper. Using a small paddle or cutting board, carefully place pizza on parchment in preheated pan, letting excess parchment extend over sides of pan.

**2.** Bake until crust is golden brown and cheese is melted, 15 to 20 minutes. Using excess parchment as handles, remove pizza, and place on a cutting board. Let stand for 5 minutes before serving. Garnish with basil, if desired.

# EVERYTHING ROLLS

**MAKES 16**

*If you're a fan of everything bagels, you'll go nuts over this fluffy take that's packed with sunflower, poppy, flax, sesame, and fennel seeds.*

**ROLLS**

- 2⅓ cups all-purpose flour
- 1⅓ cups whole wheat flour
- 1 cup warm water (105° to 110°)
- ¼ cup warm whole milk (105° to 110°)
- ¼ cup honey
- 2 tablespoons unsalted butter, softened
- 2 teaspoons kosher salt
- 2 teaspoons active dry yeast
- ½ teaspoon onion powder
- 1 cup sunflower seeds
- 2½ tablespoons poppy seeds, divided
- 2 tablespoons flax seeds
- 1 large egg
- 1 teaspoon water
- 1½ teaspoons sesame seeds
- 1 teaspoon fennel seeds
- 1 teaspoon garlic salt
- 1 teaspoon diced onion flakes
- ½ teaspoon flaked sea salt

**GREEN ONION SPREAD**

- 4 ounces cream cheese, softened
- ½ cup unsalted butter, softened
- ¼ cup chopped green onion
- 1 teaspoon kosher salt
- ½ teaspoon ground black pepper

**FOR ROLLS**

**1.** In the bowl of a stand mixer fitted with the dough hook attachment, stir together flours, 1 cup warm water, warm milk, honey, butter, kosher salt, yeast, and onion powder. Beat at medium speed until a smooth and elastic dough has formed, about 5 minutes, stopping to scrape sides of bowl. On low speed, beat in sunflower seeds, 2 tablespoons poppy seeds, and flax seeds until combined.

**2.** Turn out dough onto a lightly floured surface, and knead 5 times. Shape dough into a ball. Spray a large bowl with cooking spray; add dough, turning to grease top. Cover with plastic wrap, and let stand in a warm, draft-free place (75°) until doubled in size, about 1 hour.

**3.** Spray a 12-inch cast-iron skillet with cooking spray. Divide dough into 16 pieces; shape into balls. Place 1 inch apart in a 12-inch cast-iron skillet. Cover and let stand in a warm, draft-free place (75°) until doubled in size, about 15 minutes.

**4.** Preheat oven to 375°. In a small bowl, whisk together egg and 1 teaspoon water. In another small bowl, stir together sesame seeds, fennel seeds, garlic salt, onion flakes, sea salt, and remaining ½ tablespoon poppy seeds. Brush egg mixture onto rolls; sprinkle with seed mixture.

**5.** Bake until golden brown, about 25 minutes. Let cool in pan on wire rack for 15 minutes. Serve warm with Green Onion Spread.

**FOR SPREAD**

**1.** In a medium bowl, stir together cream cheese, butter, green onion, salt, and pepper. Cover and refrigerate for up to 5 days.

# BUTTERNUT SQUASH AND KALE FLATBREAD

**MAKES 4 SERVINGS**

*This homemade flatbread tastes like delicious restaurant fare but is made with store-bought pizza dough.*

- ¾ pound butternut squash, peeled and thinly sliced
- 3 tablespoons olive oil, divided
- 1 teaspoon kosher salt
- ½ teaspoon ground black pepper
- 1 (16-ounce) bag deli pizza dough, room temperature
- ¼ cup thinly sliced red onion
- 1 cup chopped fresh kale
- ¼ cup crumbled feta cheese
- ¼ cup pecan halves, toasted
- 1 tablespoon chopped fresh sage

Garnish: flaked sea salt, olive oil

**1.** Preheat oven to 425°. Line a rimmed baking sheet with foil.
**2.** In a large bowl, toss together squash, 1 tablespoon oil, kosher salt, and pepper. Arrange squash in a single layer on prepared pan.
**3.** Bake until tender, 14 to 16 minutes. Remove squash from pan.
**4.** Line pan with parchment paper. Shape pizza dough into a large oval on pan. Brush with 1 tablespoon oil. Top with onion, cooked squash, and kale. Drizzle with remaining 1 tablespoon oil.
**5.** Bake for 15 minutes. Remove from oven, and sprinkle with feta, pecans, and sage. Sprinkle with sea salt, and drizzle with oil, if desired.

Imperial
STAINLESS USA

# SPICY SWEET POTATO BREAD

**MAKES 1 LOAF**

*This bread is a great way to use leftover mashed sweet potatoes.*

- **1 cup cooked mashed sweet potato**
- **¾ cup warm water (105° to 110°)**
- **¼ cup firmly packed light brown sugar**
- **3¼ cups bread flour**
- **1 tablespoon instant yeast**
- **2 teaspoons kosher salt**
- **¾ teaspoon ground chipotle chile pepper**
- **Garnish: smoked paprika**

**1.** In the bowl of a stand mixer fitted with the dough hook attachment, stir together sweet potato, ¾ cup warm water, and brown sugar.

**2.** In a large bowl, whisk together flour, yeast, salt, and chile pepper. With mixer on low speed, add flour mixture to sweet potato mixture, beating until just until combined, stopping to scrape sides of bowl. Increase speed to medium-high, and beat until a smooth dough forms, about 15 minutes, stopping to scrape sides of bowl.

**3.** Turn out dough onto a lightly floured surface, and shape into a ball. (Dough may be sticky; use additional flour if needed.) Spray a large bowl with cooking spray. Place dough in bowl, turning to grease top. Cover with plastic wrap, and let stand in a warm, draft-free place (75°) until doubled in size, about 1 hour.

**4.** Place a 6- to 8-quart oval cast-iron Dutch oven with lid in oven; preheat oven to 425°.

**5.** Turn out dough onto a lightly floured piece of parchment paper. Divide dough into thirds; shape each portion into a 12-inch-long rope. Pinch ropes together at one end; braid ropes, and pinch opposite ends together. Gently tuck both pinched ends slightly under braid. Loosely cover with plastic wrap; let stand for 20 minutes.

**6.** Carefully transfer braided dough on parchment to hot Dutch oven; cover with lid. Bake until bread is golden brown, about 25 minutes. Let cool in pot for 10 minutes. Remove bread on parchment, and let cool completely on a wire rack. Garnish with smoked paprika, if desired. Store in an airtight container for up to 3 days.

# NO-KNEAD DUTCH OVEN BREAD

**MAKES 1 LOAF**

*Rustic and perfectly imperfect, this no-fuss bread features a crispy crust and chewy interior.*

- **3 cups all-purpose flour**
- **2 teaspoons kosher salt**
- **1 teaspoon active dry yeast**
- **1½ cups warm water (105° to 110°)**

**1.** In a large bowl, whisk together flour, salt, and yeast. Stir in 1½ cups warm water until combined. (Dough will be wet.) Cover bowl tightly with plastic wrap, and let stand in a warm, draft-free place (75°) until dough bubbles and flattens on top, 10 to 18 hours.

**2.** Preheat oven to 450°. Place a 4- to 6-quart cast-iron Dutch oven covered with lid in oven to preheat for 30 minutes.

**3.** Sprinkle a large sheet of parchment paper generously with flour. Place dough on paper, and quickly shape into a ball; generously sprinkle top of dough with flour. Loosely cover dough with plastic wrap; let stand for30 minutes.

**4.** Carefully remove preheated pot from oven. Transfer parchment with dough to pot. Cover with lid.

**5.** Bake for 45 minutes. Remove lid, and bake until golden brown, about 10 minutes more. Carefully remove bread from pot, and let cool completely on a wire rack before slicing.

# BUTTERMILK CHEDDAR AND CHIVE BREAD

**MAKES 1 (9X5-INCH) LOAF**

*Soft and buttery in texture, this braided loaf is perfect sliced and eaten warm or used for a lavish grilled cheese sandwich.*

- **3 cups all-purpose flour**
- **¼ cup sugar**
- **2¾ teaspoons instant yeast**
- **2 teaspoons kosher salt**
- **4 large eggs, divided**
- **2 egg yolks**
- **⅔ cup warm whole buttermilk (120° to 130°)**
- **¾ cup unsalted butter, softened**
- **1½ cups shredded Cheddar cheese**
- **⅓ cup chopped fresh chives**
- **⅓ cup chopped green onion**
- **1 tablespoon water**

**1.** Spray a 9x5-inch loaf pan with cooking spray.
**2.** In the bowl of a stand mixer fitted with the paddle attachment, combine flour, sugar, yeast, and salt. With mixer on low speed, add 3 eggs, egg yolks, and warm buttermilk, beating until mixture comes together, 2 to 3 minutes. (If mixture remains too dry and crumbly, add more buttermilk, 1 tablespoon at a time.) Increase mixer speed to medium-high, and beat for 6 minutes.
**3.** Switch to the dough hook attachment. With mixer on medium speed, add butter in three additions, letting each addition incorporate before adding the next. Increase mixer speed to medium-high, and beat until a smooth and elastic dough forms and pulls away from sides of bowl. (If dough does not pull away from bowl, add more flour, 1 tablespoon at a time.)
**4.** In a small bowl, combine cheese, chives, and green onion. In another small bowl, whisk together 1 tablespoon water and remaining 1 egg.
**5.** Turn out dough onto a heavily floured surface, and divide into 3 equal portions. Working with one portion at a time, roll dough into a 16x12-inch rectangle. Brush one long side of dough with egg wash. Sprinkle one-third of cheese mixture over dough. Starting at opposite long side, roll up dough, jelly roll style; pinch seam to seal. Place on a sheet pan. Repeat twice with remaining dough and remaining cheese mixture. Braid all three ropes together, and tuck ends under. Place braid in prepared pan. Cover and let rise in a warm, draft-free place (75°) until doubled in size, 1 hour and 30 minutes to 2 hours. (Alternatively, dough can be made 1 day in advance, and refrigerated overnight before rolling and filling.)
**6.** Preheat oven to 350°.
**7.** Brush top of dough with remaining egg wash.
**8.** Bake for 30 minutes. Loosely cover with foil, and bake until an instant-read thermometer inserted in center registers 190°, about 25 minutes more. Let cool in pan for 15 minutes. Remove from pan, and let cool on a wire rack. Serve slightly warm.

# ROSEMARY FOCACCIA

**MAKES 2 (9-INCH) SKILLETS**

*With olive oil, fresh rosemary, sea salt, and a crispy golden crust, this skillet focaccia is a warm and fragrant treat.*

**1 cup warm water (105° to 110°)**
**2 tablespoons sugar**
**1 (0.25-ounce) package active dry yeast**
**2½ cups all-purpose flour**
**1½ teaspoons kosher salt**
**8 tablespoons olive oil, divided**
**¼ cup chopped fresh rosemary, divided**
**Garnish: sea salt, ground black pepper**

**1.** In a medium bowl, stir together 1 cup warm water, sugar, and yeast; let stand until frothy and bubbling, about 5 minutes.
**2.** In the bowl of a stand mixer fitted with the paddle attachment, combine flour and salt. With mixer at low speed, add yeast mixture and melted butter, stirring just until combined. Switch to the dough hook attachment. Beat at medium speed until dough is smooth and elastic, about 7 minutes.
**3.** Spray a large bowl with cooking spray. Place dough in bowl, turning to grease top. Cover and let rise in a warm, draft-free place (75°) until doubled in size, about 1 hour.
**4.** Drizzle 2 tablespoons oil into a 18x13-inch rimmed sheet pan (or 2 (9-inch) cast-iron skillets).
**5.** Lightly punch down dough. Add 2 tablespoons rosemary, kneading until combined. Place in prepared pan, pressing into bottom of pan. Cover and let rise in a warm, draft-free place (75°) until doubled in size, about 45 minutes.
**6.** Preheat oven to 375°. Using your fingertips, press dough to create divots. Sprinkle with remaining 2 tablespoons rosemary, and drizzle with remaining 2 tablespoons oil.
**7.** Bake, uncovered, until golden brown, about 20 minutes. Garnish with sea salt and pepper, if desired.

# IRISH CHEDDAR WHITE SODA BREAD

**MAKES 1 (10-INCH) LOAF**

*The grand symbol of Ireland's baking, Irish soda bread is defined not by the baking soda but by the soft white wheat that grows in Ireland. Slashed with a cross and pricked to release heat–or fairies?–our traditional soda bread is enhanced with strong Irish Cheddar, fresh dill, and ground black pepper.*

- **3⅔ cups all-purpose flour**
- **1½ teaspoons kosher salt**
- **½ teaspoon baking soda**
- **1 cup course grated Irish aged white Cheddar cheese, divided**
- **1 tablespoon chopped fresh dill**
- **½ teaspoon ground black pepper**
- **2 cups whole buttermilk**

**1.** Preheat oven to 450°F.

**2.** In a large bowl, whisk together flour, salt, and baking soda until well combined. Stir in ⅔ cup cheese, dill, and pepper. Make a well in center, and add buttermilk. Using your hand like a claw, mix buttermilk into dry ingredients, working from center to outside of bowl, just until combined and a ball of dough forms. (Dough should be sticky and clumpy.)

**3.** Turn out dough onto a lightly floured surface. Using floured hands, gently shape into a round. Turn dough over, and tuck and rotate dough until edges are rounded and even. Transfer to a sheet of parchment paper. Pat into a 1½-inch-thick disk. Using a knife dipped in flour, cut a 1-inch-deep "X" across top of dough. Using tip of knife, prick a hole into each of the four sections of dough. Sprinkle remaining ⅓ cup cheese on top. Transfer on parchment paper to a baking sheet.

**4.** Bake for 15 minutes. Reduce oven temperature to 400°F, and bake until golden brown and an instant-read thermometer inserted in a section of bread registers 200°F, 15 to 20 minutes more. (If you tap bottom of loaf, it should sound hollow.) Remove from pan, and place on a wire rack. Let cool enough to handle, about 30 minutes. Best served warm.

# GRUYÈRE, ONION & PEPPER BISCUITS

**MAKES 16**

*The secret to the flakiest, fluffiest buttermilk biscuits is cold ingredients and a quick layering process. Once formed, our shaggy dough is swiftly quartered and stacked, creating unmistakable layers that lead to tall and flaky biscuits. In this savory recipe, nutty Gruyère cheese, dried minced onion, and spicy black pepper make these biscuits heavenly.*

- **4 cups all-purpose flour**
- **2 tablespoons granulated sugar**
- **1½ tablespoons baking powder**
- **4 teaspoons kosher salt**
- **1 tablespoon dried minced onion**
- **1½ teaspoons ground black pepper**
- **¼ teaspoon baking soda**
- **1 cup cold unsalted butter, cubed**
- **1⅓ cups shredded Gruyère cheese, divided**
- **1½ cups cold whole buttermilk**
- **1 tablespoon (14 grams) unsalted butter, melted**

**1.** Preheat oven to 425°F. Line a baking sheet with parchment paper.

**2.** In a large bowl, whisk together flour, sugar, baking powder, salt, onion, pepper, and baking soda. Add cold butter, and toss to coat. Using a pastry blender or 2 forks, cut in butter until mixture is crumbly and butter is pea-size. Stir in 1 cup cheese. Add cold buttermilk. Stir with a fork until shaggy dough forms.

**3.** Turn out dough onto a lightly floured surface, and pat into a 9-inch square (about 1 inch thick). (Dough will be crumbly.) Using a bench scraper, cut dough in quarters. Stack quarters, and pat or roll into a 9-inch square. Repeat procedure twice. Using a knife or bench scraper dipped in flour, cut dough into 16 (2¼-inch) squares. Place at least ½ inch apart on prepared pan. Freeze for 15 minutes.

**4.** Brush tops of dough with melted butter, and sprinkle with remaining ⅓ cup cheese.

**5.** Bake until golden brown, 16 to 18 minutes. Serve hot.

# FARMSTAND CORNBREAD

**MAKES 1 (10-INCH) LOAF**

*We loaded this masterpiece with all our harvest favorites for one pretty and delicious cornbread.*

- 3 tablespoons plus ½ teaspoon canola oil, divided
- 2¼ cups chopped kale, divided
- 2 cups plain yellow cornmeal
- 1 cup all-purpose flour
- 2¾ teaspoons kosher salt, divided
- 2 teaspoons garlic powder
- ½ teaspoon baking powder
- ½ teaspoon baking soda
- 2 cups whole buttermilk
- 2 large eggs, lightly beaten
- 3 tablespoons unsalted butter, melted
- 1 cup shredded extra-sharp Cheddar cheese, plus more for sprinkling
- 2 (4-ounce) jars diced pimientos, drained and divided
- ⅓ cup finely chopped jalapeño
- ½ small red onion, peeled and cut lengthwise into ¼-inch-thick wedges
- ½ cup halved pickled okra, patted dry
- 1 small jalapeño, stemmed and sliced into ¼-inch-thick rounds
- ¼ teaspoon ground black pepper

**1.** Preheat oven to 425°.

**2.** In a 10-inch cast-iron skillet, heat 1 tablespoon oil over medium heat. Add 2 cups kale; cook, stirring occasionally, until wilted and crisp-tender, 5 to 6 minutes. Transfer kale to a small bowl, and let cool for 10 minutes.

**3.** To skillet, add 2 tablespoons oil; place in oven until very hot, about 8 minutes.

**4.** In a large bowl, whisk together cornmeal, flour, 2½ teaspoons salt, garlic powder, baking powder, and baking soda. In another large bowl, whisk together buttermilk, eggs, and melted butter. Make a well in center of cornmeal mixture; whisk in buttermilk mixture just until combined. Stir in cooled kale, cheese, 1 jar pimientos, and chopped jalapeño. Carefully spread batter into hot skillet.

**5.** In a small bowl, toss together remaining ¼ cup kale and remaining ½ teaspoon oil. Sprinkle kale mixture, onion, okra, sliced jalapeño, and remaining jar of pimientos on top of batter. Sprinkle with pepper and remaining ¼ teaspoon salt.

**6.** Bake until a wooden pick inserted in center comes out clean, 25 to 30 minutes, loosely covering with foil to prevent kale from overbrowning.

**7.** Sprinkle with additional cheese, if desired. Bake until cheese is melted, about 3 minutes more. Let cool in pan on a wire rack for 15 minutes before serving.

# ROSEMARY CHEDDAR BREAD

**MAKES 1 (8X4-INCH) LOAF**

*Herbaceous and cheesy, this quick bread will be everyone's new favorite indulgence.*

- **1 cup whole milk, room temperature**
- **½ cup sour cream, room temperature**
- **¼ cup unsalted butter, melted and slightly cooled**
- **1 large egg, room temperature**
- **3 cups all-purpose flour**
- **1½ cups shredded Cheddar cheese**
- **1½ tablespoons baking powder**
- **1½ tablespoons chopped fresh rosemary**
- **2 teaspoons kosher salt**
- **⅛ teaspoon ground red pepper**

**1.** Preheat oven to 350°F. Butter an 8x4-inch loaf pan.

**2.** In a large bowl, whisk together milk, sour cream, melted butter, and egg. Add flour, Cheddar, baking powder, rosemary, salt, and red pepper, stirring just until dry ingredients are combined. Spoon batter into prepared pan.

**3.** Bake until a wooden pick inserted in center comes out clean, 1 hour and 30 minutes to 1 hour and 40 minutes. Let cool in pan for 10 minutes. Serve warm or at room temperature.

# BUTTERMILK BISCUITS

**MAKES 12**

*These perfect biscuits are rich, buttery, flaky, and ready for your favorite filling.*

- **3½ cups all-purpose flour***
- **2 tablespoons sugar**
- **1 tablespoon kosher salt**
- **1 tablespoon baking powder**
- **½ teaspoon baking soda**
- **1¼ cups cold unsalted butter, cubed**
- **1 cup cold whole buttermilk**
- **1 large egg, beaten**
- **Flaked sea salt**

**1.** Preheat oven to 425°. Line a baking sheet with parchment paper.

**2.** In a large bowl, stir together flour, sugar, salt, baking powder, and baking soda. Using two forks or a pastry blender, cut in cold butter until mixture is crumbly. Stir in cold buttermilk just until a shaggy dough forms.

**3.** Turn out dough onto a lightly floured surface. Pat dough into a rectangle, and cut into fourths. Stack each fourth on top of each other, and pat down into a rectangle again. Repeat process 3 more times. Pat or roll dough 1 inch thick. Using a 2½-inch round cutter dipped in flour, cut dough without twisting cutter, rerolling scraps as necessary. Place biscuits 2 inches apart on prepared pan. Freeze until cold, about 10 minutes. Brush with egg; sprinkle with sea salt.

**4.** Bake until golden brown, about 15 minutes.

**We used White Lily.*

# PUMPKIN-PARMESAN BREAD

**MAKES 2 (8X4-INCH) LOAVES**

*Parmesan and sage pair perfectly with pumpkin in this savory and slightly sweet quick bread.*

- **3½ cups all-purpose flour**
- **1⅓ cups sugar**
- **1½ teaspoons kosher salt**
- **1 teaspoon baking soda**
- **1 teaspoon baking powder**
- **1 teaspoon ground ginger**
- **½ teaspoon ground black pepper**
- **5 large eggs, lightly beaten**
- **1¼ cups canola oil**
- **1 (15-ounce) can pumpkin**
- **1 cup grated Parmesan cheese, divided**
- **½ cup chopped fresh sage**

**1.** Preheat oven to 350°. Spray 2 (8x4-inch) loaf pans with baking spray with flour.

**2.** In a large bowl, stir together flour, sugar, salt, baking soda, baking powder, ginger, and pepper. Add eggs and oil, stirring until well combined. Stir in pumpkin, ¾ cup Parmesan, and sage. Divide batter between prepared pans. Sprinkle with remaining ¼ cup Parmesan.

**3.** Bake until a wooden pick inserted in center comes out clean, 1 hour to 1 hour and 5 minutes.

# PARKER HOUSE ROLLS

**MAKES ABOUT 48**

*Named for the Parker House Hotel in Boston where they originated in the 1870s, these buttery rolls go well with any Southern spread.*

- **1½ cups whole milk, divided**
- **¼ cup sugar**
- **2 teaspoons active dry yeast**
- **4 to 4½ cups all-purpose flour, divided**
- **6 tablespoons unsalted butter, melted, plus more for brushing**
- **2 large eggs**
- **1 tablespoon kosher salt**
- **½ cup plus 1 teaspoon unsalted butter, softened and cut into 48 cubes**

**1.** In a small bowl, whisk together ½ cup milk, sugar, and yeast. Let stand until mixture is foamy, about 10 minutes. Stir ½ cup flour into yeast mixture.

**2.** In the bowl of a stand mixer fitted with the dough hook attachment, beat melted butter, eggs, and remaining 1 cup milk at low speed until combined. Add yeast mixture, beating to combine. Add 1 cup flour and salt; beat to combine. Gradually add remaining 3 cups flour, one cup at a time, beating until dough comes together and begins to pull away from sides of bowl, 2 to 3 minutes. (Dough will be sticky. If dough is too sticky, add more flour, ¼ cup at a time, until it comes together.)

**3.** Spray a large bowl with cooking spray. Place dough in bowl, turning to grease top. Cover and let stand in a warm, draft-free place (75°) until doubled in size, 2 hours to 2 hours and 30 minutes.

**4.** On a lightly floured surface, turn out dough. Divide dough in half, and gently shape each half into a ball. Cover and let rest for 10 minutes.

**5.** Spray 2 (12-inch) cast-iron skillets with cooking spray. Roll one half of dough into a 14x12-inch rectangle, about ¼ inch thick. Using a 2½-inch round cutter, cut dough, rerolling scraps as needed. Repeat with remaining dough.

**6.** Brush each circle with melted butter, and place one cube of softened butter on bottom half of each one. Fold circles over, and press to seal. Place in prepared skillets. Cover and let stand in a warm, draft-free place (75°) until puffed, about 30 minutes.

**7.** Preheat oven to 350°. Brush rolls with melted butter, and bake until golden brown, 20 to 25 minutes. Brush with additional melted butter.

# PASTA

*chapter 3*

# CREAMY ORECCHIETTE WITH WINTER GREENS

**MAKES 4 SERVINGS**

*This hearty pasta dish makes an ideal meal for any day of the week. The curved surface of orecchiette soaks up every bit of the creamy cheese sauce, while winter greens add nourishment and sustenance.*

- 2 tablespoons olive oil
- 6 cloves garlic, finely chopped
- 3 cups water
- 2 cups vegetable stock
- 1 (16-ounce) package orecchiette
- ¾ teaspoon kosher salt
- ½ teaspoon ground black pepper
- 4 cups torn Swiss chard leaves, large stems removed
- 4 cups torn Lacinato kale leaves, large stems removed
- ½ cup freshly grated pecorino cheese, plus more to serve
- ¼ cup heavy whipping cream

**1.** In a Dutch oven, heat oil over medium heat. Add garlic; cook until fragrant, about 2 minutes. Add 3 cups water, stock, pasta, salt, and pepper; bring to a simmer. Reduce heat to medium; cook for 5 minutes, stirring occasionally. Add greens; cook, stirring occasionally, until pasta is al dente, 7 to 9 minutes. Remove from heat; add pecorino and cream. Sprinkle with additional salt, if desired. Serve immediately with additional pecorino.

# PANCETTA CARBONARA

**MAKES 6 SERVINGS**

*Carbonara lovers, rejoice! We've revamped this classic, creamy pasta dish by balancing out the cream and cheese with low-sodium chicken broth so you can enjoy it in all of its glory with none of the guilt.*

- **1½ cups diced pancetta**
- **4 cloves garlic, minced**
- **1 (32-ounce) container low-sodium chicken broth**
- **½ teaspoon kosher salt**
- **1 (12-ounce) package bucatini pasta**
- **2 large eggs**
- **¾ cup shredded Parmesan cheese**
- **½ cup heavy whipping cream**
- **3 tablespoons chopped fresh sage**
- **¼ teaspoon ground black pepper**

**Garnish: chopped fresh sage, shredded Parmesan cheese, ground black pepper**

**1.** Heat a large Dutch oven over medium heat. Add pancetta; cook, stirring occasionally, until crisp, about 12 minutes. Remove pancetta using a slotted spoon, and let drain on paper towels.
**2.** Add garlic to Dutch oven; cook until fragrant, about 30 seconds. Add broth and salt; cover and bring to a boil. Add pasta; cover and cook for 7 minutes.
**3.** In a small bowl, whisk together eggs, Parmesan, and cream. Gradually stir egg mixture into pasta mixture; simmer until thickened, about 2 minutes.
**4.** Stir in pancetta, sage, and pepper. Garnish with sage, Parmesan, and pepper, if desired.

# BAKED ZITI

**MAKES 6 SERVINGS**

*Peas add a pop of color and fresh flavor to this cheesy, mouthwatering pasta. Essentially the adult version of the baked ziti you grew up eating at Sunday supper, this meal is, without question, one everyone in the family can get behind.*

- **2 tablespoons olive oil**
- **1 pound ground beef**
- **1½ teaspoons kosher salt, divided**
- **2 cloves garlic, finely chopped**
- **1 (28-ounce) can crushed tomatoes**
- **3 cups water**
- **1 (16-ounce) package ziti**
- **2 teaspoons chopped fresh oregano**
- **1 cup frozen peas, thawed**
- **¾ cup whole-milk ricotta cheese**
- **1 (8-ounce) bag shredded mozzarella cheese**

**1.** Preheat oven to broil.
**2.** In a deep, ovenproof 12-inch skillet, heat oil over medium heat. Add beef and ½ teaspoon salt; cook, stirring occasionally, until browned and crumbly, about 5 minutes. Add garlic; cook for 1 minute. Increase heat to medium-high. Add tomatoes, 3 cups water, pasta, oregano, and remaining 1 teaspoon salt; bring to a simmer, stirring frequently. Reduce heat to medium; cook, stirring frequently, until pasta is al dente, about 9 minutes. Remove from heat; stir in peas and ricotta. Top with mozzarella.
**3.** Broil until golden, about 2 minutes. Let cool for 5 minutes; serve warm.

# PASTA PRIMAVERA

**MAKES 6 SERVINGS**

*Celebrate fresh, flavorful produce with a pasta dinner starring tender asparagus, sweet green peas, and summer squash.*

- 2 tablespoons unsalted butter
- 1 medium yellow squash, halved lengthwise and sliced ¼ inch thick crosswise
- 1 large red bell pepper, seeded and diced
- 1 cup thinly sliced red onion
- 2 cloves garlic, thinly sliced
- 1 (32-ounce) carton vegetable broth
- ¼ cup dry white wine, such as Pinot Grigio or sauvignon blanc
- ½ teaspoon kosher salt
- ½ teaspoon ground black pepper
- ¼ teaspoon crushed red pepper
- 1 (16-ounce) package angel-hair pasta
- 2 cups chopped fresh asparagus
- 1 cup fresh or thawed frozen peas
- 1 cup shredded Parmesan cheese
- ½ cup chopped fresh parsley

Garnish: crushed red pepper, fresh parsley

**1.** In a 6-quart cast-iron Dutch oven, melt butter over medium-high heat. Add squash, bell pepper, onion, and garlic; cover and cook, stirring occasionally, until vegetables are tender, about 6 minutes.

**2.** Stir in broth, wine, salt, black pepper, and red pepper; bring to a boil. Stir in pasta; reduce heat to medium, and cook, stirring occasionally, until pasta is tender, 8 to 10 minutes, adding asparagus and peas during last 3 minutes of cooking. Stir in cheese and parsley. Garnish with red pepper and parsley, if desired.

# CHICKEN FLORENTINE

**MAKES 6 SERVINGS**

*You won't miss a bite thanks to the orecchiette, which translates to "little ear" in Italian—it expertly cradles the earthy medley of mushrooms, hearty rainbow chard, and juicy chicken thighs.*

- **2 tablespoons unsalted butter**
- **1 pound boneless skinless chicken thighs, cut into ½-inch cubes**
- **1 (4-ounce) package fresh gourmet-blend mushrooms**
- **1 bunch rainbow chard, stems and leaves separated and chopped**
- **1 tablespoon all-purpose flour**
- **1 (32-ounce) container low-sodium chicken broth**
- **½ cup half-and-half**
- **1¼ teaspoons kosher salt**
- **½ teaspoon ground black pepper**
- **1 (12-ounce) package orecchiette pasta**

**Garnish: ground black pepper**

**1.** In a 12-inch saucepan, heat butter over medium-high heat. Add chicken; cook for 10 minutes. Add mushrooms and chard stems; cook for 5 minutes. Stir in flour; cook for 1 minute.

**2.** Gradually whisk in broth, half-and-half, salt, and pepper; bring to a boil. Add pasta; reduce heat to medium. Cover and cook for 12 minutes.

**3.** Remove from heat; stir in chard leaves until wilted. Garnish with pepper, if desired.

# BUCATINI PUTTANESCA WITH SPINACH AND CHICKPEAS

**MAKES 4 SERVINGS**

*Spinach and chickpeas are new additions to this essential Italian dish, which hits all the right notes thanks to the saltiness from the olives, capers, and anchovy paste that is perfectly balanced by the natural sweetness from crushed tomatoes.*

- 2 tablespoons olive oil
- 3 cloves garlic, chopped
- 2 teaspoons anchovy paste
- 1 (28-ounce) can crushed tomatoes
- 1 (12-ounce) package bucatini
- 3 cups water
- 1 teaspoon kosher salt
- 1 (15-ounce) can chickpeas, rinsed and drained
- 1 (5-ounce) bag fresh baby spinach, large stems removed
- ¾ cup pitted kalamata olives, chopped
- 3 tablespoons drained brined capers

**1.** In a deep 12-inch skillet, heat oil over medium heat. Add garlic and anchovy paste; cook for 2 minutes. Add tomatoes, pasta, 3 cups water, and salt; bring to a simmer. Cook, stirring occasionally, until pasta is al dente, 9 to 11 minutes.

**2.** Reduce heat to low. Add chickpeas, spinach, olives, and capers; cover and cook for 2 minutes. Stir gently to combine. Serve immediately.

# BAKED CAVATAPPI AND BRUSSELS SPROUTS ALFREDO

**MAKES 4 SERVINGS**

*Smoky bacon and melted cheese pack scrumptious flavor into this creamy baked pasta.*

- **4** slices thick-cut bacon, chopped
- **¾** pound Brussels sprouts, halved
- **1** cup chopped red onion
- **2** cloves garlic, minced
- **½** pound cavatappi, cooked according to package directions
- **1** (15-ounce) jar four-cheese Alfredo sauce
- **1** cup shredded Gruyère cheese (4 ounces), divided
- **1** (4-ounce) jar diced pimiento, drained
- **½** teaspoon kosher salt
- **½** teaspoon ground black pepper

**1.** Preheat oven to 375°.
**2.** In a large cast-iron skillet, cook bacon over medium heat until crisp, 8 to 10 minutes. Remove bacon using a slotted spoon, and let drain on paper towels, reserving drippings in skillet.
**3.** Add Brussels sprouts and onion to pan; cook over medium-high heat until lightly browned, about 6 minutes. Add garlic; cook for 1 minute. Remove from heat; stir in cooked pasta, Alfredo sauce, ½ cup cheese, pimiento, salt, pepper, and bacon until combined.
**4.** Spoon pasta mixture into 4 (6-inch) cast-iron baking dishes; sprinkle with remaining ½ cup cheese. Place dishes on a rimmed baking sheet.
**5.** Bake until hot and bubbly, about 20 minutes. Let stand for 10 minutes before serving.

# CASARECCE WITH PANCETTA AND WHITE BEANS

**MAKES 4 SERVINGS**

*If crispy pancetta, hearty cannellini beans, and a considerable amount of freshly grated Parmesan cheese aren't reason enough to add this pasta to your weeknight meal rotation, the fact that it cooks in under 30 minutes will be.*

- **2 tablespoons olive oil**
- **1 (4-ounce) package diced pancetta**
- **1 cup chopped yellow onion**
- **1 (28-ounce) can diced tomatoes**
- **1 (16-ounce) package casarecce**
- **2 cups chicken broth**
- **2 teaspoons chopped fresh rosemary**
- **¾ teaspoon kosher salt**
- **½ teaspoon crushed red pepper**
- **1 (15-ounce) can cannellini beans, rinsed and drained**
- **½ cup freshly grated Parmesan cheese, plus more to serve**

**1.** In a Dutch oven, heat oil over medium heat. Add pancetta; cook until golden and crisp, about 5 minutes. Remove pancetta using a slotted spoon; set aside. Add onion and cook for 4 minutes, stirring occasionally.

**2.** Add tomatoes, pasta, broth, rosemary, salt, and red pepper to Dutch oven; bring to a simmer. Cook, stirring occasionally, until pasta is al dente, about 12 minutes. Add beans; cook for 1 minute. Remove from heat; stir in cheese and reserved pancetta. Serve immediately with additional cheese, if desired.

# SAUSAGE AND FENNEL PAPPARDELLE

**MAKES ABOUT 4 SERVINGS**

*Pecorino cheese adds the perfect salty finish to this simple pasta dish.*

- **3¼ teaspoons kosher salt, divided**
- **1 (8.8-ounce) package pappardelle**
- **1 tablespoon olive oil**
- **1 pound sweet Italian sausage, casings removed**
- **1 medium yellow onion, thinly sliced**
- **1 large fennel bulb, cored and thinly sliced, fronds reserved**
- **½ teaspoon ground black pepper**
- **1 cup low-sodium chicken broth**
- **1 cup freshly grated pecorino cheese**
- **½ cup heavy whipping cream**
- **Garnish: freshly grated pecorino cheese, chopped fennel fronds**

**1.** In a large Dutch oven, bring 4 inches water and 3 teaspoons salt to a boil over medium-high heat. Add pasta; cook until tender, about 4 minutes. Drain well.

**2.** In a large cast-iron skillet, heat oil over medium-high heat. Add sausage; cook until browned, about 5 minutes. Remove sausage using a slotted spoon, and let drain on paper towels.

**3.** Add onion to skillet; cook, stirring occasionally, until tender, about 8 minutes. Stir in fennel, pepper, and remaining ¼ teaspoon salt; reduce heat to medium. Cook, stirring occasionally, until fennel is softened and onion is golden, about 5 minutes. Add sausage and broth; cook, stirring frequently, until heated through, about 2 minutes. Add pasta to sausage mixture, tossing to coat. Stir in cheese and cream. Garnish with cheese and fennel fronds, if desired.

# COUSCOUS WITH PEAS AND PANCETTA

**MAKES 6 SERVINGS**

*While some argue that couscous is neither a pasta nor a grain, there's no arguing over this stunning flavor combination. Laden with peas, pancetta, and sugar snaps, this bowl of goodness gets finished with a dollop of ricotta cheese, a sprinkle of fresh mint, and a generous drizzle of olive oil for good measure.*

- **8 ounces diced pancetta**
- **12 ounces Israeli couscous**
- **1 cup fresh or frozen green peas**
- **8 ounces sugar snap peas, cut into thirds**
- **3 tablespoons fresh lemon juice**
- **½ teaspoon kosher salt, plus more to taste**
- **¼ teaspoon ground black pepper**
- **½ cup roughly torn fresh mint leaves, divided**
- **½ cup whole-milk ricotta cheese**
- **1 teaspoon lemon zest**

**Garnish: olive oil**

**1.** Heat a large skillet over medium heat. Add pancetta; cook, stirring frequently with a wooden spoon, until golden and crispy, 8 to 10 minutes. Remove using a slotted spoon, and let drain on paper towels, reserving ¼ cup drippings in skillet.

**2.** Bring a large pot of salted water to a boil over high heat. Add couscous; cook for 5 minutes. Add green peas and snap peas; cook for 2 minutes. Reserve 2 tablespoons pasta water. Drain pasta, and transfer to skillet with drippings. Add reserved 2 tablespoons pasta water, lemon juice, salt, and pepper, stirring to combine. Return to low heat; cook until most of pasta water is absorbed and sauce is silky, about 1 minute. Fold in half of pancetta and ¼ cup mint. Transfer to serving bowls. Top with ricotta, lemon zest, remaining pancetta, and remaining ¼ cup mint. Garnish with oil, if desired.

# CREAMY LEMON CHICKEN PASTA

**MAKES 6 SERVINGS**

*Spiral-shaped fusilli hold on to the goat cheese and Parmesan sauce exceptionally well, packing each bite full of flavor.*

- **1 tablespoon olive oil**
- **1 pound boneless skinless chicken breasts, cut into ½-inch pieces**
- **1¼ teaspoons kosher salt**
- **1 teaspoon ground black pepper**
- **1 (32-ounce) carton low-sodium chicken broth**
- **3 sprigs fresh basil**
- **2 cloves garlic, thinly sliced**
- **1 large lemon, zested and juiced**
- **1 (16-ounce) package fusilli**
- **1 cup shredded Parmesan cheese**
- **½ cup crumbled goat cheese**
- **2 cups fresh baby spinach**

**Garnish: lemon zest, crumbled goat cheese, ground black pepper**

**1.** In a 12-inch enamel-coated cast-iron braiser, heat oil over medium-high heat. Add chicken, salt, and pepper; cook, stirring occasionally, until lightly browned, about 5 minutes.

**2.** Add broth, basil, garlic, and lemon zest; bring to a boil. Add pasta; cover and cook, stirring occasionally, until tender, about 10 minutes. Discard basil.

**3.** Add Parmesan, goat cheese, and lemon juice, stirring until combined. Stir in spinach until wilted. Garnish with lemon zest, goat cheese, and pepper, if desired.

# LOADED MAC AND CHEESE

**MAKES 10 TO 12 SERVINGS**

*We love how the super-cheesy sauce clings to every nook and cranny of the pasta in this crowd-pleaser.*

- **¼ cup unsalted butter**
- **½ cup all-purpose flour**
- **1 clove garlic, minced**
- **2 teaspoons kosher salt**
- **1 teaspoon Worcestershire sauce**
- **½ teaspoon dry mustard**
- **½ teaspoon ground black pepper**
- **4 cups whole milk**
- **1 cup sour cream**
- **4 cups shredded Colby-Jack cheese blend, divided**
- **1 (16-ounce) package cavatappi, cooked according to package directions**
- **4 tablespoons chopped fresh chives, divided**
- **½ cup panko (Japanese bread crumbs)**
- **4 slices thick-cut bacon, cooked and crumbled**
- **2 tablespoons unsalted butter, melted**

**1.** Preheat oven to 350°.

**2.** In a 12-inch cast-iron skillet, melt butter over medium heat. Whisk in flour, garlic, salt, Worcestershire, mustard, and pepper; cook for 2 minutes. Whisk in milk and sour cream until smooth; bring to a simmer. Cook, stirring constantly, until thickened, about 4 minutes. Whisk in 3½ cups cheese until melted. Stir in cooked pasta and 2 tablespoons chives until combined.

**3.** In a small bowl, stir together bread crumbs, bacon, melted butter, remaining ½ cup cheese, and remaining 2 tablespoons chives. Sprinkle over pasta mixture.

**4.** Bake until golden brown and bubbly, 15 to 20 minutes. Let stand for 10 minutes before serving.

# SOUTHERN-STYLE PEANUT NOODLES

**MAKES 4 TO 6 SERVINGS**

*Accented with hot sauce, thick-cut bacon, and collard greens, these peanut noodles are a fun take on a classic Thai dish. meal rotation, the fact that it cooks in under 30 minutes will be.*

## NOODLES

- ⅔ cup creamy peanut butter
- ½ cup water
- 2 tablespoons distilled white vinegar
- 1 tablespoon hot sauce
- 1½ teaspoons sugar
- ¾ teaspoon kosher salt, divided
- 6 slices thick-cut bacon
- 1 pound large fresh shrimp, peeled and deveined (tails left on)
- 6 cups (½-inch-thick) sliced fresh collard greens
- 2 cloves garlic, finely chopped
- ½ pound linguini, cooked according to package directions
- ¼ cup chopped salted cocktail peanuts

## QUICK PICKLED CUCUMBERS

- 1 cup thinly sliced cucumber
- 1 cup thinly sliced onion
- 2 tablespoons distilled white vinegar
- 1 tablespoon sugar
- 1 teaspoon vegetable oil
- ¼ teaspoon kosher salt

## FOR NOODLES

**1.** In a medium bowl, whisk together peanut butter, ½ cup water, vinegar, hot sauce, sugar, and ½ teaspoon salt until smooth.

**2.** In a large skillet, cook bacon over medium heat until crisp. Remove bacon, and let drain on paper towels, reserving drippings in skillet. Increase heat to medium-high.

**3.** In a large bowl, toss together shrimp and remaining ¼ teaspoon salt. Add shrimp to skillet; cook, turning occasionally, until pink and firm, 4 to 5 minutes. Remove from skillet.

**4.** Add collard greens and garlic to skillet; cook until greens are wilted, 2 to 3 minutes. Remove from heat. Add cooked pasta, shrimp, and peanut butter mixture, tossing gently to coat. Sprinkle with peanuts. Crumble bacon, and sprinkle over pasta mixture. Serve with Quick Pickled Cucumbers.

## FOR CUCUMBERS

**1.** In a medium bowl, toss together all ingredients. Cover and let stand for at least 1 hour or refrigerate for up to 3 days.

# CREAMY MUSHROOM AND GOAT CHEESE GNOCCHI

**MAKES 4 SERVINGS**

*This vegetarian-friendly pasta dish is every bit as luscious and soul-warming as it sounds. A variety of mushrooms adds texture and a punch of umami flavor that contrasts perfectly with tangy goat cheese and white wine.*

- **4 tablespoons olive oil, divided**
- **12 ounces gourmet blend fresh fresh gourmet-blend mushrooms**
- **½ teaspoon kosher salt**
- **¼ teaspoon ground black pepper**
- **¼ cup diced shallot**
- **½ cup white wine**
- **2 cups vegetable broth**
- **1 (16-ounce) package gnocchi***
- **1 tablespoon chopped fresh thyme leaves**
- **1 (4-ounce) package goat cheese, crumbled and divided**

**Garnish: chopped fresh thyme**

**1.** In a 12-inch skillet, heat 3 tablespoons oil over medium-high heat. Add mushrooms in a single layer; cook for 2 minutes. Sprinkle mushrooms with salt and pepper, stirring to combine; cook for 2 minutes. Push mushrooms to one side of skillet. Add remaining 1 tablespoon oil to skillet. Add shallot; cook for 1 minute. Stir together mushrooms and shallot.

**2.** Stir in wine, scraping browned bits from bottom of skillet with a wooden spoon; cook until wine is reduced by half, about 1 minute. Add broth, gnocchi, and thyme; bring to a simmer. Cook, stirring gently, until gnocchi are softened, 3 to 4 minutes.

**3.** Remove from heat; stir in 3 ounces goat cheese. Top with remaining 1 ounce goat cheese. Sprinkle with additional salt and pepper, if desired. Garnish with thyme, if desired. Serve immediately.

**We used Gia Russa Gnocchi with Potato.*

# FUSILLI ROMESCO WITH SHRIMP

**MAKES 6 SERVINGS**

*Curly pasta expertly grasps every bit of this mouthwatering, homemade romesco sauce. Whether it's served cold or hot, we have no doubt this dish will quickly become a go-to meal.*

- **1 pound large fresh shrimp, peeled and deveined (tails left on)**
- **⅓ cup plus 2 tablespoons olive oil, divided**
- **1 tablespoon lemon zest**
- **1 teaspoon kosher salt, divided, plus more to taste**
- **¼ teaspoon ground black pepper**
- **1 (16-ounce) jar roasted red peppers, drained**
- **⅓ cup Marcona almonds**
- **2 tablespoons fresh lemon juice**
- **2 tablespoons sherry vinegar**
- **3 cloves garlic**
- **1 teaspoon smoked paprika**
- **1 (16-ounce) package fusilli**
- **½ cup loosely packed fresh parsley leaves**
- **Garnish: roughly chopped Marcona almonds**

**1.** Place shrimp in a medium bowl. Add 2 tablespoons oil, lemon zest, ½ teaspoon salt, and black pepper, stirring to combine. Cover and refrigerate for 15 minutes.

**2.** To make romesco: In the work bowl of a food processor, place roasted peppers, Marcona almonds, lemon juice, vinegar, garlic, paprika, and remaining ½ teaspoon salt; purée until almost smooth, about 1 minute. With processor running, add remaining ⅓ cup oil in a slow, steady stream until combined.

**3.** Heat a large cast-iron Dutch oven over medium heat. Place shrimp on pan in a single layer; cook until pink and firm, about 2 minutes per side. Transfer to a plate; set aside.

**4.** In the same Dutch oven, bring salted water to a boil over high heat. Add pasta; cook until al dente, about 9 minutes. Reserve ¾ cup pasta water. Drain pasta, and return to pot.

**5.** Add reserved ¾ cup pasta water and romesco sauce to pasta, stirring well to combine. Return to medium-low heat; cook for 2 minutes. Transfer to a serving bowl. Top with shrimp and parsley. Garnish with Marcona almonds, if desired.

# ITALIAN MAC AND CHEESE

**MAKES 6 TO 8 SERVINGS**

*Sun-dried tomatoes add a note of sweetness to this sausage-packed pasta.*

**½ cup oil-packed sun-dried tomatoes**
**1 pound mild Italian sausage**
**3 cloves garlic, thinly sliced**
**1 tablespoon all-purpose flour**
**½ teaspoon kosher salt**
**½ teaspoon ground black pepper**
**½ teaspoon crushed red pepper**
**3 cups half-and-half**
**2 cups shredded Asiago cheese**
**1 (16-ounce) package ziti, cooked according to package directions**
**½ cup chopped fresh basil**
**Garnish: fresh basil leaves**

**1.** Drain sun-dried tomatoes, reserving 2 tablespoons oil, and chop; set aside.
**2.** In a 12-inch enamel-coated cast-iron braiser, heat reserved 2 tablespoons sun-dried tomato oil over medium-high heat. Add sausage; cook until browned, about 8 minutes. Remove sausage using a slotted spoon, and let drain on paper towels.
**3.** Add sun-dried tomatoes and garlic to braiser; cook for 1 minute. Whisk in flour, salt, black pepper, and red pepper; cook for 1 minute. Gradually whisk in half-and-half until smooth; bring to a simmer. Gradually whisk in cheese until smooth. Stir in cooked pasta, basil, and sausage; cook until heated through, about 3 minutes. Garnish with basil, if desired.

# MEDITERRANEAN SHRIMP ORZOTTO

**MAKES 4 SERVINGS**

*This take on risotto—made with orzo instead of traditional Arborio rice—showcases a delightful combination of fresh dill, lemon, and feta cheese that brightens up this sumptuous one-pot seafood pasta.*

- **4 tablespoons olive oil, divided**
- **1 pound large fresh shrimp, peeled and deveined (tails left on)**
- **¾ teaspoon kosher salt, divided**
- **1 cup diced yellow onion**
- **1 (16-ounce) package orzo**
- **2½ cups water**
- **2 cups light chicken broth**
- **1 cup cherry tomatoes, halved**
- **1 cup pitted Castelvetrano olives, chopped**
- **2 tablespoons fresh lemon juice**
- **½ cup crumbled feta cheese**
- **¼ cup chopped fresh dill**

**1.** In a deep 12-inch skillet, heat 2 tablespoons oil over medium-high heat. Add shrimp in a single layer; sprinkle with ¼ teaspoon salt. Cook for 3 minutes, turning once. Remove shrimp from skillet; set aside.

**2.** Reduce heat to medium, and add remaining 2 tablespoons oil to skillet. Add onion and remaining ½ teaspoon salt; cook until onion is slightly translucent, about 4 minutes. Add pasta, and stir to coat with oil; cook for 2 minutes. Add 2½ cups water and broth; cook for 12 minutes, stirring constantly.

**3.** Reduce heat to low. Stir in shrimp, tomatoes, and olives; cook for 1 minute. Remove from heat; add lemon juice. Top with feta, and dill. Serve immediately.

# MAINS

## chapter 4

# WHITE WINE ROAST CHICKEN

**MAKES 4 SERVINGS**

*All the great things about spatchcocking a chicken—an even doneness throughout, crispy skin, and less cook time—are made better when roasted alongside earthy parsnips coated in white wine, garlic, and fresh herbs.*

- **1 cup dry white wine**
- **3 tablespoons olive oil**
- **1½ teaspoons kosher salt**
- **1½ teaspoons ground black pepper**
- **1 (3- to 4-pound) whole chicken, backbone removed**
- **2 pounds parsnips, peeled and quartered lengthwise**
- **5 cloves garlic, smashed**
- **5 sprigs fresh thyme**
- **5 sprigs fresh rosemary**
- **5 sprigs fresh oregano**
- **Garnish: fresh thyme sprigs, fresh rosemary sprigs, fresh oregano sprigs**

**1.** Preheat oven to 450°.
**2.** Line a 17½x12½-inch rimmed baking sheet with parchment paper.
**3.** In a large bowl, stir together wine, oil, salt, and pepper. Add chicken, turning to coat. Place chicken on prepared pan, pressing firmly on breast bone to flatten. Add parsnips and garlic to wine mixture, turning to coat. Add parsnips, garlic, and wine mixture to prepared pan. Add thyme, rosemary, and oregano.
**4.** Bake for 25 minutes. Reduce oven temperature to 430° and bake until a meat thermometer inserted in thickest portion registers 165°, about 20 minutes more. Garnish with thyme, rosemary, and oregano, if desired.

# SALMON CAESAR GRAIN BOWL

**MAKES 4 SERVINGS**

*Wholesome and well-rounded, this filling meal is perfectly balanced by a creamy Caesar dressing.*

- **4 (6-ounce) salmon fillets**
- **1 tablespoon olive oil**
- **½ teaspoon kosher salt**
- **½ teaspoon ground black pepper**
- **2 romaine hearts, chopped**
- **1 cup red quinoa, cooked according to package directions**
- **½ cup shaved Parmesan cheese**
- **½ cup Caesar dressing**

**1.** Preheat oven to 325°. Line a rimmed baking sheet with foil.
**2.** Place salmon on prepared pan. Drizzle with 1 tablespoon olive oil, and sprinkle with ½ teaspoon salt and ¼ teaspoon ground black pepper.
**3.** Roast for 20 minutes.
**4.** Divide lettuce among 4 serving bowls. Add ½ cup cooked quinoa to each bowl. Top each with Parmesan and a salmon fillet. Drizzle each with 2 tablespoons Caesar dressing, and sprinkle with black pepper. Serve immediately.

# PORK FRICASSEE

MAKES 4 SERVINGS

*If you like smothered pork chops, you'll love this Southern twist on a classic French stew.*

- 4 (6-ounce) pork loin chops, 1 inch thick
- 2 teaspoons kosher salt, divided
- ½ teaspoon ground black pepper
- ½ teaspoon ground red pepper
- ¾ cup all-purpose flour, divided
- ¼ cup salted butter
- ½ cup vegetable oil
- ¼ pound applewood-smoked bacon, diced
- 1 cup chopped yellow onion
- 1 cup chopped red bell pepper
- ½ cup chopped celery
- 8 ounces fresh cremini mushrooms, quartered
- 2 cloves garlic, minced
- 2 teaspoons chopped fresh thyme
- 2 dried bay leaves
- 2 cups chicken stock
- ½ cup dry white wine
- Hot cooked rice, to serve
- Garnish: chopped green onions, fresh thyme leaves

**1.** Sprinkle pork chops with 1 teaspoon salt and ground peppers. Place ¼ cup flour in a shallow dish; dredge chops in flour.

**2.** In a large Dutch oven, melt butter over medium heat. Add pork chops and brown on both sides. Remove pork chops from pot.

**3.** To pot, add oil and remaining ½ cup flour. Cook over medium-high heat, stirring constantly, until mixture is dark brown in color, about 20 minutes. Add bacon; cook for 1 minute. Add onion, bell pepper, celery, mushrooms, garlic, thyme, bay leaves, and remaining 1 teaspoon salt; stir well. Stir in stock and wine. Return pork chops to pot, placing in an even layer.

**4.** Bring to a boil; reduce heat and simmer until pork chops are tender, about 1 hour.

**5.** Remove pork chops and keep warm. Increase heat to medium; cook, uncovered, until sauce is thickened, about 10 minutes. Serve over rice. Garnish with green onion and thyme, if desired.

# INDIAN BUTTER CHICKEN

**MAKES 6 SERVINGS**

*Packed with flavor, this vibrant meal can be on the dinner table in 20 minutes. You'll want plenty of naan on hand to soak up every drop!*

- ½ cup unsalted butter
- 2 pounds boneless skinless chicken thighs, cut into bite-size pieces
- 1 cup chopped yellow onion
- 6 cloves garlic, minced
- 1 cup strained tomatoes*
- 1 cup heavy whipping cream
- 1 tablespoon minced fresh ginger
- 2 teaspoons garam masala
- 1½ teaspoons kosher salt
- 1½ teaspoons chili powder
- 1½ teaspoons ground cumin
- Hot cooked rice and toasted naan, to serve
- Garnish: chopped fresh cilantro

**1.** Select SAUTÉ feature on Instant Pot. Add butter to pot, and heat until melted. Add chicken, onion, and garlic; sauté until outside of chicken is no longer pink, about 3 minutes. Select CANCEL feature.
**2.** Add tomatoes, cream, ginger, garam masala, salt, chili powder, and cumin. Cover and lock lid. Select MANUAL feature. Pressure cook on LOW for 5 minutes. Quick release pressure. Serve over hot cooked rice with naan. Garnish with cilantro, if desired.

**We used Pomi.*

# BEEF FAJITAS

**MAKES 4 TO 6 SERVINGS**

*Turn dinner into a spiced-up celebration with these colorful, flavorful fajitas. Feel free to get creative with your toppings and let everyone build their own.*

**8** **small flour tortillas**
**6** **tablespoons vegetable oil, divided**
**5¼** **teaspoons organic fajita seasoning, divided**
**3½** **cups (¼-inch) sliced assorted bell peppers**
**3** **cups (¼-inch) sliced red onion (about 1 large onion)**
**1** **pound flank steak, cut against the grain into ¼-inch-thick slices**
**1** **clove garlic, grated**
**1** **jalapeño, thinly sliced (about 1 ounce)**
**¼** **cup packed chopped fresh cilantro**
**Lime wedges and sour cream, to serve**
**Garnish: chopped fresh cilantro**

**1.** Position oven rack in top third of oven and preheat oven to broil. Place a 17½x12½-inch rimmed baking sheet in oven to preheat. Wrap tortillas in foil; set aside.

**2.** In a large bowl, combine 2 tablespoons oil and 2 teaspoons fajita seasoning. Add bell peppers and onion; toss to combine. Carefully remove pan from oven; add vegetable mixture, spreading in an even layer.

**3.** Broil until vegetables are crisp-tender, 8 to 10 minutes.

**4.** In same bowl, toss together steak, garlic, remaining 4 tablespoons oil, and remaining 3¼ teaspoons fajita seasoning. Move vegetable mixture, clearing one-third of pan; add steak. Sprinkle jalapeño over vegetables. On side opposite to steak, push vegetable mixture, clearing one corner of pan; add wrapped tortillas.

**5.** Broil until steak is browned and cooked to desired degree of doneness, 4 to 6 minutes. Drain any excess juices, if needed. Sprinkle cilantro over steak and vegetables; toss to combine. Serve with lime wedges and sour cream. Garnish with cilantro, if desired.

# CHICKEN SHIITAKE MARSALA

MAKES 2 SERVINGS

*We've taken this Italian American dish and added our own flair. We love the rich flavor of the shiitake mushroom with the mildly sweet Marsala wine.*

- **2 (6-ounce) boneless skinless chicken breasts**
- **½ teaspoon kosher salt**
- **½ teaspoon ground black pepper**
- **2 tablespoons olive oil, divided**
- **2 cups sliced fresh shiitake mushrooms**
- **¾ cup Marsala wine**
- **1 tablespoon chopped fresh oregano**
- **2 tablespoons unsalted butter**

**Garnish: chopped fresh oregano**

**1.** Season chicken with ½ teaspoon kosher salt and ¼ teaspoon ground black pepper.

**2.** In a large saucepan, heat 1 tablespoon olive oil over medium-high heat. Add chicken; cook, turning once, until golden brown and a food thermometer inserted in thickest portion registers 165°, 7 to 8 minutes per side. Remove from pan; cover with foil.

**3.** Add remaining 1 tablespoon olive oil and mushrooms to pan; cook, stirring frequently, until tender, about 2 minutes. Add wine and oregano; cook for 1 minute, scraping browned bits from bottom of pan. Remove from heat; add butter; stirring until melted. Return chicken to pan, turning to coat in sauce. Garnish with oregano, if desired.

# MONGOLIAN BEEF

**MAKES 6 SERVINGS**

*Satisfy your takeout cravings in the comfort of your own kitchen with our take on this quintessential Asian dish.*

- **2 pounds flank steak, thinly sliced**
- **⅓ cup cornstarch**
- **½ cup firmly packed dark brown sugar**
- **½ cup beef broth**
- **½ cup soy sauce**
- **¼ cup hoisin sauce**
- **6 cloves garlic, minced**
- **1 teaspoon minced fresh ginger**
- **2½ tablespoons light sesame oil**
- **1 cup julienned carrot**
- **Hot cooked rice, to serve**
- **Garnish: thinly sliced green onion, toasted sesame seeds**

**1.** In a large bowl, combine steak and cornstarch; toss well to coat. Set aside.

**2.** In a medium bowl, stir together brown sugar, broth, soy sauce, hoisin sauce, garlic, and ginger until well combined.

**3.** Select SAUTÉ feature on Instant Pot. Add oil to pot, and heat until hot. Add steak; sauté until no longer pink on the outside, about 2 minutes. Select CANCEL feature.

**4.** Add brown sugar mixture to pot. Cover and lock lid. Select MANUAL feature. Pressure cook on HIGH for 10 minutes. Quick release pressure. Uncover and stir in carrot. Partially cover pot. Let stand until carrot starts to wilt, about 5 minutes. Serve beef and carrot over hot cooked rice. Garnish with green onion and sesame seeds, if desired.

# HOISIN-BARBECUE BAKED CHICKEN

MAKES ABOUT 6 SERVINGS

*Traditional barbecue chicken just got a much-needed facelift. And that hoisin sauce you bought for one recipe and forgot you had—it's about to have coveted real estate in your refrigerator door once you taste this simple, baked chicken.*

- **1 tablespoon vegetable oil**
- **4 skinless chicken drumsticks**
- **4 bone-in skinless chicken thighs**
- **2 bone-in skinless chicken breasts**
- **1 teaspoon kosher salt**
- **½ teaspoon ground black pepper**
- **¾ cup hoisin sauce***
- **¾ cup barbecue sauce**
- **⅓ sliced green onion**
- **2 teaspoons toasted sesame seeds**

**1.** Preheat oven to 375°. Brush bottom of a roasting pan with oil.
**2.** Place chicken in prepared pan; sprinkle with salt and pepper. In a small bowl, whisk together hoisin sauce and barbecue sauce. Pour over chicken.
**3.** Bake until a meat thermometer inserted in thickest portion of chicken registers 170°, 45 to 50 minutes, occasionally spooning sauce over chicken. Let stand for 10 minutes before serving. Sprinkle with green onion and sesame seeds.

**We used Dynasty Hoisin Sauce.*

# SALMON WITH LEMON-TARRAGON BROCCOLINI

**MAKES 4 SERVINGS**

*Keep your shopping list short and cleanup simple with this easy-to-prepare sheet-pan dinner. You'll love the way tarragon's distinct anise flavor perfectly rounds out this light and bright dish.*

- **1 lemon, zested and juiced**
- **½ cup olive oil**
- **2 tablespoons chopped fresh tarragon**
- **4 cloves garlic, minced**
- **2½ teaspoons kosher salt, divided**
- **¾ teaspoon ground black pepper, divided**
- **½ pound fresh Broccolini or broccoli rabe, trimmed and halved lengthwise**
- **1 medium leek, quartered and cut into 3-inch sections**
- **1 lemon, thinly sliced**
- **4 (6-ounce) salmon fillets, skin removed**

**Garnish: chopped fresh tarragon**

**1.** Preheat oven to 450°. Line a 17½x12½-inch rimmed baking sheet with parchment paper.
**2.** In a large bowl, whisk together lemon zest and juice, oil, tarragon, garlic, 2 teaspoons salt, and ½ teaspoon pepper. Add Broccolini and leek, stirring to coat. Place in an even layer on one half of prepared pan; add lemon slices.
**3.** Sprinkle salmon with remaining ½ teaspoon salt and remaining ¼ teaspoon pepper; place on other half of pan.
**4.** Bake until salmon is firm to touch and vegetables are tender, about 15 minutes. Garnish with tarragon, if desired.

# ASIAN CHICKEN TACOS

MAKES ABOUT 4 TO 8 SERVINGS

*Inspired by the Vietnamese sandwich, bahn mi, these tacos will have you counting and recounting the number of ingredients because the flavor punch you get with each bite is created with only a few ingredients.*

**1 (9.2-ounce) package flour tortillas**
**2½ tablespoons olive oil**
**4 cups shredded cooked chicken**
**½ cup hoisin sauce**
**1 medium carrot, peeled and julienned**
**2 tablespoons chopped fresh cilantro**
**¼ teaspoon kosher salt**
**¼ teaspoon ground black pepper**
**Garnish: fresh cilantro leaves**

**1.** Preheat oven to 350°.
**2.** Wrap tortillas in a damp paper towel, then wrap in foil. Place in oven until warmed, about 15 minutes.
**3.** In a large saucepan, heat 1 tablespoon olive oil over medium-high heat. Add chicken and hoisin sauce; cook, stirring occasionally, until heated through, about 5 minutes.
**4.** In a small bowl, stir together carrot, cilantro, 1½ teaspoons olive oil, ¼ teaspoon kosher salt, and ¼ teaspoon ground black pepper. Serve chicken in warmed tortillas with carrot mixture. Garnish with cilantro, if desired.

# GRILLED FLANK STEAK WITH CHIMICHURRI SAUCE

MAKES 6 TO 8 SERVINGS

*Pile this flavorful flank steak onto your favorite tortillas and top with Chimichurri Sauce, thinly sliced radish, sliced avocado, and crumbled queso fresco for delicious tacos.*

**FLANK STEAK**

- **1½ pounds flank steak**
- **2 tablespoons firmly packed light brown sugar**
- **1 tablespoon chili powder**
- **1 tablespoon garlic powder**
- **2 teaspoons kosher salt**
- **1½ teaspoons ground black pepper**
- **1 teaspoon dry mustard**
- **1 teaspoon ground cumin**

**CHIMICHURRI SAUCE**

- **½ cup finely chopped parsley**
- **½ cup olive oil**
- **2 tablespoons red wine vinegar**
- **1 tablespoon minced shallot**
- **3 cloves garlic, grated**
- **2 teaspoons finely chopped fresh oregano**
- **1¼ teaspoons kosher salt**
- **1 teaspoon lemon zest**
- **¼ teaspoon crushed red pepper**

**FOR STEAK**

**1.** Let steak stand at room temperature for 30 minutes.

**2.** In a small bowl, stir together brown sugar, chili powder, garlic powder, salt, pepper, mustard, and cumin. Generously sprinkle mixture all over steak; let stand 15 minutes more.

**3.** Heat a large cast-iron grill pan over medium-high heat; spray pan with cooking spray.

**4.** Cook steak, turning once, until an instant-read thermometer inserted in the thickest part registers at least 130°, 10 to 15 minutes, or until desired doneness. Transfer to a cutting board, and let stand for 10 minutes. Slice steak diagonally against the grain. Serve with Chimichurri Sauce.

**FOR SAUCE**

**1.** In a medium bowl, whisk together all ingredients. Cover and let stand at room temperature for at least 15 minutes before serving.

# BUTTERMILK-BRINED CHICKEN

MAKES 4 TO 6 SERVINGS

*Get ready to meet your new favorite way to prepare chicken! Using buttermilk tenderizes the meat without toughening it, and packs a serious flavor punch.*

- **1 (32-ounce) container whole buttermilk**
- **5½ teaspoons kosher salt, divided**
- **1½ teaspoon ground black pepper, divided**
- **4 bone-in skin-on chicken quarters**
- **10 sprigs fresh tarragon**
- **1 (24-ounce) package baby Dutch potatoes, halved**
- **1 bunch radishes, trimmed and halved**
- **1 tablespoon olive oil**

**Garnish: chopped fresh tarragon**

**1.** In a large bowl, whisk together buttermilk, 4 teaspoons kosher salt, and 1 teaspoon ground black pepper. Add chicken and tarragon, turning to coat. Cover and refrigerate for at least 4 hours or overnight.

**2.** Preheat oven to 425°.

**3.** Drain chicken, discarding tarragon. Pat chicken dry with paper towels. Place in an even layer on a 17½x12½-inch rimmed baking sheet.

**4.** In a large bowl, stir together potatoes, radishes, 1 tablespoon olive oil, remaining 1½ teaspoons kosher salt, and remaining ½ teaspoon ground black pepper. Place potato mixture around chicken.

**5.** Bake for 25 minutes. Reduce oven temperature to 400°, and bake until vegetables are tender and an instant-read thermometer inserted in thickest portion of chicken registers 165°, about 20 minutes more. Let stand for 10 minutes before serving. Garnish with tarragon, if desired.

# SHEET-PAN SHRIMP BOIL

**MAKES 4 SERVINGS**

*Shrimp, sausage, potatoes, corn—
what's not to love about this hearty recipe?*

- **1½ pounds small gold potatoes**
- **2 tablespoons kosher salt**
- **2 heads garlic, tops cut off**
- **2 lemons, halved**
- **1 (16-ounce) package smoked sausage, diagonally sliced**
- **3 ears corn, shucked and cut into 2-inch pieces**
- **1 pound jumbo fresh shrimp, peeled and deveined (tails left on)**
- **1 tablespoon Cajun seasoning*, divided**
- **½ cup unsalted butter, melted**

**Garnish: chopped fresh parsley, sliced fresh chives**

**1.** Preheat oven to 425°. Line a rimmed baking sheet with foil. Place one oven rack in the center position and one oven rack in the upper third position.

**2.** In a medium pot, combine potatoes, salt, and cold water to cover. Bring to a boil over medium-high heat; cook until just fork tender, about 10 minutes. Drain potatoes.

**3.** Cut potatoes in half and place on prepared pan, cut side down. Place garlic, cut side down, and lemons, cut side up, on pan. Bake on the center rack until potatoes are lightly golden and begin to crisp, about 15 minutes. Add sausage and corn to pan; bake until sausage is crisp and corn has started to brown, 15 to 20 minutes more.

**4.** Add shrimp to pan and sprinkle 2 teaspoons Cajun seasoning over everything. Bake on the upper rack until shrimp are firm, pink, and cooked through, 7 to 10 minutes more.

**5.** Squeeze the roasted garlic and lemons into a small bowl and stir together pulp and juice until well combined. Add melted butter and remaining 1 teaspoon Cajun seasoning, stirring until well combined. Serve immediately with shrimp boil. Garnish with parsley and chives, if desired.

**We used Slap Ya Mama Cajun Seasoning.*

# STUFFED POBLANO PEPPERS

MAKES 6 SERVINGS

*Stuffed with seasoned black beans, rice, and plenty of cheese, these peppers are an easy all-in-one supper.*

**3 large poblano peppers, halved and seeded**
**½ cup yellow corn kernels**
**¼ cup chopped red onion**
**1 tablespoon olive oil**
**2 cloves garlic, minced**
**1 plum tomato, diced**
**½ cup long-grain rice, cooked according to package directions**
**½ cup rinsed and drained black beans**
**½ cup cubed Monterey Jack cheese with peppers**
**¼ cup chopped fresh cilantro**
**½ teaspoon kosher salt**
**½ teaspoon ground cumin**
**2 tablespoons crumbled goat cheese**
**Garnish: chopped fresh cilantro**

**1.** Preheat oven to broil.
**2.** Heat a 12-inch cast-iron skillet over high heat. Add poblanos; cook, turning frequently, until charred on all sides, about 5 minutes. Remove from skillet. Add corn and onion to skillet; cook, stirring occasionally, until charred, about 3 minutes. Add oil and garlic; cook until garlic is fragrant, about 1 minute.
**3.** In a large bowl, stir together corn mixture, tomato, cooked rice, beans, Monterey Jack, cilantro, salt, and cumin until combined. Place charred peppers in skillet. Spoon corn mixture into pepper halves. Sprinkle with goat cheese.
**4.** Broil until cheese is melted, 2 to 3 minutes. Garnish with cilantro, if desired.

10

LODGE
1896

# TORTILLA CHICKEN PIE

**MAKES 1 (10-INCH) PIE**

*Whip up this tasty, satisfying supper in no time at all.*

**PIE**
- 4 cups shredded cooked chicken
- 1 cup fresh corn kernels
- ½ cup diced red onion
- ¼ cup diced jalapeño
- 2 teaspoons kosher salt
- 1 teaspoon ground black pepper
- ½ teaspoon ground cumin
- ¼ teaspoon chili powder
- 12 (6-inch) corn tortillas
- 1 (16-ounce) jar mild tomatillo salsa
- 3 cups shredded sharp Cheddar cheese, plus additional to serve

Garnish: fresh cilantro, sour cream

**CORN PICO DE GALLO**
- ½ cup fresh corn kernels
- ½ cup diced tomatoes
- ¼ cup diced red onion
- 2 tablespoons diced jalapeño
- 2 teaspoons fresh lime juice
- 1 teaspoon kosher salt
- 1 teaspoon chopped fresh cilantro
- ¼ teaspoon ground cumin

## FOR PIE

**1.** Preheat oven to 375°. Lightly grease a 10-inch cast-iron skillet.

**2.** In a large bowl, toss together chicken, corn, onion, and jalapeño. Add salt, black pepper, cumin, and chili powder.

**3.** Lay 4 tortillas in the prepared dish, overlapping as needed. Spread half of the chicken mixture over the tortillas. Top with half of tomatillo salsa, about ¾ cup, and 1 cup shredded cheese. Repeat layers once. Top with remaining 4 tortillas and remaining 1 cup shredded cheese. Cover with lightly greased foil.

**4.** Bake until pie is golden and the cheese is melted and bubbly, 20 to 30 minutes. Let cool for 5 minutes before serving. Serve with Corn Pico de Gallo. Garnish with cilantro, sour cream, and cheese, if desired.

## FOR PICO DE GALLO

**1.** In a small bowl, toss together corn, tomatoes, onion, and jalapeño. Add lime juice, salt, cilantro, and cumin. Serve immediately or store in the refrigerator until ready to serve. Store in an airtight container in the refrigerator for up to 3 days.

# PAN-SEARED PORK CHOPS WITH MUSTARD GRAVY

MAKES 4 SERVINGS

*Searing with lard creates a deep-brown crust on the chops and helps produce a rich sauce.*

**1¾ teaspoons kosher salt**
**1 teaspoon garlic powder**
**½ teaspoon ground black pepper**
**4 (7-ounce) bone-in pork rib chops (about ¾ inch thick)**
**2 tablespoons lard**
**½ cup finely chopped red onion**
**4 cloves garlic, minced**
**⅔ cup apple cider vinegar**
**¾ cup low-sodium chicken broth**
**¼ cup apple juice**
**1 tablespoon coarse-ground Dijon mustard**
**1 teaspoon chopped fresh sage**
**Garnish: fresh sage leaves**

**1.** In a small bowl, stir together salt, garlic powder, and pepper; sprinkle all over pork chops. Refrigerate, uncovered, on a wire rack set over a rimmed baking sheet for at least 8 hours or overnight.
**2.** Rinse chops under cold water, and thoroughly pat dry with paper towels. Let stand at room temperature for 30 minutes.
**3.** In a 12-inch cast-iron skillet, melt lard over medium-high heat. Cook pork chops in batches until browned and an instant-read thermometer inserted in the thickest part registers 145°, about 6 minutes per side. Transfer chops to a serving platter, and keep warm, reserving drippings in skillet.
**4.** Reduce heat to medium. Add onion and garlic to skillet; cook, stirring frequently, for 1 minute. Stir in vinegar; cook until reduced by half, 2 to 4 minutes. Stir in broth, juice, mustard, and any pork juices that have accumulated on platter; bring to a boil. Cook until reduced to ½ cup, about 4 minutes. Stir in sage. Spoon sauce onto pork chops. Garnish with sage, if desired. Serve immediately.

# SHEET-PAN CHICKEN POT PIE

MAKES 4 TO 6 SERVINGS

*Transformed from its traditional pie pan, we created an easy, quick-baking yet still hearty pot pie.*

- **2 tablespoons unsalted butter**
- **2 cups chopped carrot**
- **1 cup chopped celery**
- **½ cup chopped yellow onion**
- **1 clove garlic, minced**
- **1½ teaspoons kosher salt**
- **¾ teaspoon ground black pepper**
- **1 cup low-sodium chicken broth**
- **3 tablespoons all-purpose flour**
- **1½ cups heavy whipping cream**
- **3 cups shredded cooked chicken**
- **1 cup frozen peas, thawed**
- **1 tablespoon chopped fresh parsley**
- **½ (14.1-ounce) package refrigerated piecrusts, room temperature**

**Garnish: chopped fresh parsley**

**1.** Preheat oven to 400°. Place a sheet of foil on bottom rack of oven. Spray a small 13x9-inch rimmed baking sheet with cooking spray.

**2.** In a large saucepan, melt butter over medium-high heat. Add carrot, celery, onion, garlic, salt, and pepper; cook until vegetables are crisp-tender, about 5 minutes. Add broth and flour, stirring until combined. Add cream; cook, stirring occasionally, until slightly thickened, about 6 minutes. Stir in chicken, peas, and parsley. Pour mixture into prepared pan.

**3.** On a lightly floured surface, roll dough into a 16x11-inch rectangle. Cut dough into 11 (1-inch-wide) strips. Arrange dough strips in a lattice pattern on top of filling. Trim dough strips, and gently press to seal.

**4.** Bake until golden brown and bubbly, 35 to 40 minutes. Garnish with parsley, if desired.

# SHEET-PAN STEAK WITH SMOKED PAPRIKA POTATOES

MAKES 6 TO 8 SERVINGS

*If you don't have a cast-iron baking pan, sear the steaks in a 12-inch cast-iron skillet and use a traditional metal rimmed baking sheet for steps 4 through 6.*

- **2 pounds rib-eye steaks (1-inch thick)**
- **3¼ teaspoons kosher salt, divided**
- **1¼ teaspoons ground black pepper, divided**
- **¾ teaspoon garlic powder**
- **4 tablespoons vegetable oil, divided**
- **1 pound baby Yukon gold potatoes, halved**
- **¾ pound baby red potatoes, halved**
- **1 tablespoon chopped fresh oregano**
- **2 teaspoons smoked paprika**
- **6 medium green onions, roots trimmed**

**Garnish: fresh oregano**

**1.** Preheat oven to 400°. Sprinkle steaks with 1¾ teaspoons salt, ¾ teaspoon pepper, and garlic powder. Let stand at room temperature for 30 minutes.

**2.** Heat a 14-inch cast-iron baking pan on the stovetop over high heat; add 2 tablespoons oil. Carefully swirl pan to coat surface.

**3.** Pat steaks dry. Add steaks to pan; cook until browned and a crust forms, about 3 minutes per side. Remove pan from heat; transfer steaks to a plate.

**4.** In a large bowl, stir together potatoes, oregano, paprika, remaining 2 tablespoons oil, remaining 1½ teaspoons salt, and remaining ½ teaspoon pepper. Spread onto baking pan.

**5.** Bake for 10 minutes. Stir potatoes; add green onion to pan. Bake until potatoes are tender, about 15 minutes more.

**6.** Push vegetables to edge of pan; place steaks in middle, and turn once to coat in oil. Bake until a meat thermometer inserted in thickest portion of steaks reads 130° to 135° for medium-rare to medium, 3 to 5 minutes, or until steaks reach desired doneness. Let steaks stand for 10 minutes before serving. Garnish with oregano, if desired.

# CREAMY GARLIC BACON PORK CHOPS

MAKES 4 SERVINGS

*This hearty skillet main is quick enough for a weeknight but fancy enough for company.*

- **4 (8-ounce) bone-in pork chops**
- **2 teaspoons kosher salt, divided**
- **1 teaspoon ground black pepper, divided**
- **6 slices thick-cut bacon, chopped**
- **1 small yellow onion, thinly sliced**
- **4 cloves garlic, minced**
- **1½ teaspoons chopped fresh rosemary**
- **½ cup dry white wine**
- **1½ cups heavy whipping cream**
- **2 tablespoons Dijon mustard**
- **½ cup shredded Parmesan cheese**

**Garnish: chopped fresh rosemary**

**1.** Sprinkle pork chops with 1½ teaspoons salt and ½ teaspoon pepper. Let stand at room temperature for 15 minutes.

**2.** In a 12-inch cast-iron skillet, cook bacon over medium-high heat, stirring occasionally, until crisp, 10 to 12 minutes. Remove using a slotted spoon, and let drain on paper towels. Reserve 2 tablespoons drippings in skillet. Add pork chops; cook until browned, turning once, about 3 minutes per side. Remove from pan.

**3.** Add onion; cook, stirring occasionally, until tender, about 5 minutes. Add garlic and rosemary; cook until fragrant, about 1 minute. Add white wine; cook until reduced by half, about 1 minute. Stir in cream, mustard, remaining ½ teaspoon salt, and remaining ½ teaspoon pepper; bring to a simmer. Reduce heat to medium; cook, stirring occasionally, until slightly thickened, about 3 minutes. Whisk in cheese until smooth.

**4.** Add pork chops; continue cooking until a food thermometer inserted registers 150° and sauce is thickened, about 10 minutes more. Stir in bacon before serving. Garnish with rosemary, if desired.

# RATATOUILLE WITH SHRIMP

MAKES 4 TO 6 SERVINGS

*Channel the classic French dish with a sheet pan of fresh herbs, tomato paste, and a host of garden veggies.*

- **2 cups (1-inch) pieces red bell pepper**
- **2 cups (1-inch) pieces yellow bell pepper**
- **1 cup coarsely chopped carrot**
- **1 cup coarsely chopped onion**
- **3 cloves garlic, chopped**
- **4 tablespoons tomato paste, divided**
- **3 tablespoons red wine vinegar, divided**
- **3 tablespoons extra-virgin olive oil, divided**
- **1½ teaspoons kosher salt, divided**
- **¾ teaspoon ground black pepper, divided**
- **¼ teaspoon crushed red pepper**
- **6 cups (1-inch) cubed eggplant**
- **2 tablespoons chopped fresh basil**
- **1 tablespoon chopped fresh oregano**
- **1½ pounds large fresh shrimp, peeled and deveined**

**Garnish: chopped fresh oregano, chopped fresh basil**

**1.** Preheat oven to 375°. Spray a large rimmed baking sheet with cooking spray.
**2.** In a large bowl, combine bell peppers, carrot, onion, and garlic. Add 3 tablespoons tomato paste, 2 tablespoons vinegar, 2 tablespoons oil, ½ teaspoon salt, ¼ teaspoon black pepper, and crushed red pepper, tossing to coat. Spread mixture on prepared pan. Loosely cover with foil.
**3.** Bake for 20 minutes, stirring once.
**4.** In a medium bowl, combine eggplant, basil, oregano, ½ teaspoon salt, ¼ teaspoon black pepper, remaining 1 tablespoon tomato paste, remaining 1 tablespoon vinegar, and remaining 1 tablespoon oil. Add eggplant mixture to bell pepper mixture.
**5.** Bake, uncovered, until eggplant is softened, about 15 minutes, stirring once. Add shrimp; sprinkle with remaining ½ teaspoon salt and remaining ¼ teaspoon black pepper.
**6.** Bake until shrimp are pink and firm, 8 to 10 minutes. Garnish with oregano and basil, if desired.

10

# THE PERFECT ROAST CHICKEN

MAKES 4 SERVINGS

*There's nothing simpler or more delicious than a roast chicken. Follow this comfort-inducing recipe for a perfectly tender, golden-brown bird.*

- 1 tablespoon lemon zest
- 3 teaspoons kosher salt, divided
- 1 (5-pound) whole chicken, giblets removed
- ½ lemon
- 1 (16-ounce) package carrots, peeled and cut into 5-inch pieces
- 1 large sweet onion, cut into wedges
- 1 head garlic, halved
- 4 sprigs fresh thyme
- 2 tablespoons olive oil
- 1 tablespoon all-purpose flour
- 2 cups chicken broth
- ½ teaspoon ground black pepper

Garnish: fresh thyme sprigs

**1.** In a small bowl, combine zest and 2 teaspoons salt. Pat chicken dry with paper towels. Gently loosen skin from chicken, keeping skin intact. Rub salt mixture under skin and all over chicken. Place lemon half inside chicken cavity. Tie legs together with kitchen twine. Refrigerate overnight.

**2.** Preheat oven to 425°. Let chicken stand at room temperature for 30 minutes.

**3.** Place carrots, onion, garlic, and thyme in a 12-inch cast-iron skillet. Place chicken on top of vegetables. Rub chicken with oil, and sprinkle with remaining 1 teaspoon salt.

**4.** Bake until a meat thermometer inserted in thickest portion registers 165°, about 1 hour and 25 minutes, covering with foil to prevent excess browning, if necessary. Let stand for 10 minutes.

**5.** Meanwhile, remove chicken, all vegetables, and thyme from skillet; whisk in flour. Whisk in broth; cook over medium heat, whisking constantly, until thickened. Whisk in pepper. Serve gravy with chicken. Garnish with thyme, if desired.

# BAKED EGGS WITH KALE AND TOMATOES

MAKES 4 SERVINGS

*Eggs aren't just for breakfast. They are one of the simplest ingredients that can be transformed into an amazing meal. This recipe, from Amanda Frederickson, is a play on the Middle Eastern dish shakshuka, which is great any time of day. Make sure to serve some crusty bread alongside.*

**1 tablespoon olive oil**
**1 onion, diced**
**2 cloves garlic, minced**
**Kosher salt and ground black pepper, to taste**
**1 pint cherry tomatoes, diced**
**3 to 4 cups fresh kale, stemmed and chopped**
**4 large eggs**
**¼ cup feta cheese**
**Garnish: chopped fresh herbs**

**1.** Preheat oven to 425°.
**2.** In a medium ovenproof sauté pan, heat oil over medium heat. Add onion; cook until translucent, 4 to 6 minutes. Add garlic, salt, and pepper; cook for 30 seconds. Add tomatoes; cook until softened and almost falling apart, about 10 minutes. Fold in kale; sauté until wilted. Make 4 indentations in tomato mixture. Carefully crack each egg into indentations.
**3.** Bake until eggs are just set, 8 to 10 minutes. Sprinkle with feta. Garnish with herbs, if desired. Serve immediately.

# CRANBERRY-ORANGE CHICKEN

MAKES 4 SERVINGS

*With bright citrus, tart cranberries, and warm spices mingling in a sea of green beans and tender chicken breasts, this dish is sure to grace your dinner table all year long.*

- **2 large navel oranges, sliced**
- **5 tablespoons honey, divided**
- **3 tablespoons olive oil, divided**
- **2¾ teaspoons kosher salt, divided**
- **1¼ teaspoons ground black pepper, divided**
- **4 (10- to 12-ounce) bone-in skin-on chicken breasts**
- **1 pound green beans, trimmed**
- **½ cup fresh cranberries**
- **2 cloves garlic, thinly sliced**
- **1 tablespoon chopped fresh rosemary**

**Garnish: fresh rosemary**

**1.** Position oven rack in top third of oven, and preheat oven to 375°. Line a 18-x13-inch rimmed baking sheet with parchment paper.

**2.** Place orange slices in an even layer on prepared pan.

**3.** In a large bowl, whisk together 4 tablespoons honey, 2 tablespoons oil, 2 teaspoons salt, 1 teaspoon pepper, and allspice until smooth. Add chicken; stir until fully coated. Place chicken, skin side up, on top of orange slices.

**4.** Bake for 30 minutes.

**5.** In another large bowl, stir together green beans, cranberries, garlic, rosemary, remaining 1 tablespoon honey, remaining 1 tablespoon oil, remaining ¾ teaspoon salt, and remaining ¼ teaspoon pepper. Place around chicken. Bake until a food thermometer inserted in thickest portion of chicken registers 165°, about 15 minutes. Garnish with rosemary, if desired.

# DESSERTS

## chapter 5

# CHURRO AND CHOCOLATE POUND CAKE

MAKES 1 (13-CUP) CAKE

*This decadently spiced and generously drizzled cake was inspired by one of our favorite south-of-the-border sweet snacks.*

**1½ cups unsalted butter, softened**
**2 cups plus 2 tablespoons firmly packed light brown sugar, divided**
**5 large eggs, room temperature**
**2 teaspoons vanilla extract**
**3 cups all-purpose flour**
**2 teaspoons ground cinnamon, divided**
**1 teaspoon kosher salt**
**1 teaspoon baking powder**
**½ teaspoon ground nutmeg**
**1 cup sour cream**
**½ cup whole milk**
**¼ cup granulated sugar**
**2 tablespoons melted unsalted butter**
**Chocolate sauce, to serve**

**1.** Preheat oven to 350°.
**2.** In the bowl of a stand mixer fitted with the paddle attachment, beat butter and 2 cups brown sugar with a mixer at medium speed until fluffy, 2 to 3 minutes, stopping to scrape sides of bowl. Add eggs, one at a time, beating well after each addition. Beat in vanilla.
**3.** In a large bowl, whisk together flour, 1 teaspoon cinnamon, salt, baking powder, and nutmeg. In a medium bowl, whisk together sour cream and milk. With mixer on low speed, gradually add flour mixture to butter mixture alternately with sour cream mixture, beginning and ending with flour mixture, beating just until combined after each addition.
**4.** Spray a 13-cup cast-iron fluted cake pan with baking spray with flour. Spread batter into prepared pan. Gently tap pan on counter lined with a kitchen towel a few times to release air bubbles.
**5.** Bake until a wooden pick inserted near center comes out clean, about 1 hour and 10 minutes. Let cool in pan on a wire rack for 15 minutes. Invert cake onto wire rack, and let cool completely.
**6.** In a small bowl, stir together granulated sugar, remaining 2 tablespoons brown sugar, and remaining 1 teaspoon cinnamon. Working in sections, brush cake with melted butter and coat with sugar mixture, pressing gently to adhere. Serve with chocolate sauce.

# COFFEE & CREAM BLONDIES

**MAKES 1 (9-INCH) SQUARE PAN**

*These chewy squares channel the flavors of our favorite latte with chopped hazelnuts, espresso powder, and a cream cheese swirl.*

- **2 teaspoons espresso powder**
- **1 tablespoon warm water (105° to 110°)**
- **1 cup firmly packed light brown sugar**
- **1 cup unsalted butter, melted**
- **½ cup granulated sugar**
- **1¼ teaspoons vanilla extract, divided**
- **2 large eggs, room temperature**
- **2 cups all-purpose flour**
- **1½ teaspoons baking powder**
- **1 teaspoon kosher salt**
- **1 cup hazelnuts, coarsely chopped and toasted**
- **2 ounces cream cheese, softened**
- **2 tablespoons heavy whipping cream**
- **¼ cup confectioners' sugar**

**1.** In a small bowl, stir together espresso powder and 1 tablespoon warm water. Let cool completely.

**2.** Preheat oven to 350°. Spray a 9-inch square baking pan with cooking spray. Line pan with parchment paper, letting excess extend over sides of pan.

**3.** In a large bowl, whisk together espresso mixture, brown sugar, melted butter, granulated sugar, and 1 teaspoon vanilla. Add eggs, whisking well.

**4.** In a medium bowl, whisk together flour, baking powder, and salt. Gradually add flour mixture to espresso mixture, stirring just until moistened. Stir in hazelnuts. Spread batter into prepared pan.

**5.** In a large bowl, beat cream cheese with a mixer at medium speed until smooth. Beat in cream and remaining ¼ teaspoon vanilla, stopping to scrape sides of bowl. Add confectioners' sugar, beating until smooth. Drop cream cheese mixture by small spoonfuls over batter; gently swirl together with a knife.

**6.** Bake until golden brown and a wooden pick inserted in center comes out clean, 25 to 30 minutes, loosely covering with foil after 15 minutes of baking to prevent excess browning. Let cool completely on a wire rack. Using excess parchment as handles, remove from pan before cutting.

# STRAWBERRY-LEMON BUTTER CAKE

**MAKES 1 (9-INCH) CAKE**

*Not only is this stunning cake bursting with sweet, tart flavor, but it comes together in no time and adds picture-perfect color to your table.*

**½ cup unsalted butter, softened**
**1 cup granulated sugar**
**1 cup all-purpose flour**
**2 large eggs, room temperature**
**1 teaspoon lemon zest**
**1 tablespoon fresh lemon juice**
**1 teaspoon baking powder**
**¼ teaspoon fine sea salt**
**1 cup thinly sliced fresh strawberries**
**Garnish: confectioners' sugar**

**1.** Preheat oven to 350°F. Line a 9-inch round cake pan with parchment paper; spray with cooking spray.
**2.** In the bowl of a stand mixer fitted with the paddle attachment, beat butter and granulated sugar at medium speed until fluffy, 3 to 4 minutes, stopping to scrape sides of bowl. Add flour, eggs, lemon zest and juice, baking powder, and sea salt, and beat for 1 minute, stopping to scrape sides of bowl as needed. Spread batter in an even layer in prepared pan. Place strawberry slices in circles on top of batter, very gently pressing into batter.
**3.** Bake until lightly browned, 45 to 50 minutes. Run a knife around edges of pan, and let cool in pan for 15 minutes. Turn out cake onto a plate, then transfer to a serving plate, strawberries side up. Garnish with confectioners' sugar, if desired.

# LEMON BUTTERMILK CHESS PIE

**MAKES 1 (9-INCH) PIE**

*Cornmeal and buttermilk combine to create a sweet, slightly tart pie with a classic crusty top.*

- ½ (14.1-ounce) package refrigerated piecrusts
- 3 large eggs
- 1¼ cups granulated sugar
- ½ cup unsalted butter, softened
- 2 tablespoons all-purpose flour
- 1 tablespoon plain yellow cornmeal
- 1 cup whole buttermilk
- 2 teaspoons lemon zest
- 1 tablespoon fresh lemon juice
- ½ teaspoon vanilla extract
- ¼ teaspoon kosher salt
- 1 tablespoon confectioners' sugar

**1.** Preheat oven to 375°.
**2.** Unroll piecrust and place in a 9-inch pie plate, pressing into bottom and up sides. Fold edges under, and crimp as desired. Top with a sheet of parchment paper, letting ends extend over edges of plate. Add pie weights.
**3.** Bake for 15 minutes. Carefully remove paper and weights. Let cool on a wire rack for 20 minutes. Reduce oven temperature to 350°.
**4.** In a large bowl, beat eggs, granulated sugar, butter, flour, and cornmeal with a mixer at medium speed until almost smooth. Stir in buttermilk, lemon zest and juice, vanilla, and salt. Pour into prepared crust.
**5.** Bake until set, 40 to 45 minutes, covering with foil during last 10 minutes of baking to prevent excess browning, if necessary. Let cool completely. Refrigerate until chilled. Dust with confectioners' sugar before serving..

# CINNAMON-PECAN BARS

**MAKES 1 (13X9-INCH) PAN**

*This classic cinnamon-sugar cookie base takes a Southern turn with the addition of toasted pecans. Be sure to use hot caramel topping, as thinner sauces may sink while baking.*

**1 cup unsalted butter, softened**
**1½ cups sugar**
**2 large eggs, room temperature**
**1 teaspoon vanilla extract**
**2⅔ cups all-purpose flour**
**2 teaspoons ground cinnamon**
**1 teaspoon baking soda**
**1 teaspoon cream of tartar**
**½ teaspoon kosher salt**
**1 (12-ounce) jar caramel ice cream topping***
**2 cups pecan pieces**

**1.** Preheat oven to 350°. Spray a 13x9-inch baking pan with cooking spray. Line pan with parchment paper, letting excess extend over sides of pan.
**2.** In a large bowl, beat butter and sugar with a mixer at medium speed until fluffy, 3 to 4 minutes, stopping to scrape sides of bowl. Add eggs, one at a time, beating well after each addition. Beat in vanilla.
**3.** In a medium bowl, whisk together flour, cinnamon, baking soda, cream of tartar, and salt. With mixer on low speed, gradually add flour mixture to butter mixture, beating until combined. Transfer dough to prepared pan, and smooth top with an offset spatula. Spread caramel topping onto dough, and sprinkle with pecans.
**4.** Bake until a wooden pick inserted in center comes out with a few moist crumbs, 30 to 35 minutes. Let cool completely on a wire rack. Using excess parchment as handles, remove from pan, and cut into bars.

**We used Smucker's Hot Caramel Topping.*

# BANANA PUDDING

MAKES ABOUT 12 SERVINGS

*Impress your guests—and feed a crowd—with this delicious, traditional dessert.*

**PUDDING**

- **1 (14-ounce) can sweetened condensed milk**
- **1½ cups cold whole milk**
- **1 (3.4-ounce) box vanilla instant pudding mix**
- **2½ cups cold heavy whipping cream**
- **1 teaspoon vanilla extract**
- **¼ teaspoon kosher salt**
- **4 large ripe but firm bananas, sliced**
- **1 (11-ounce) box vanilla wafers**

**WHIPPED CREAM**

- **2 cups cold heavy whipping cream**
- **⅓ cup sweetened condensed milk**
- **2 teaspoons vanilla extract**
- **⅛ teaspoon kosher salt**

**Garnish: banana slices, crushed vanilla wafers**

## FOR PUDDING

**1.** In the container of a blender, process condensed milk, cold milk, and pudding mix until smooth and mixture starts to thicken, 2 to 3 minutes. Transfer to a large bowl, cover with plastic wrap, and refrigerate for 4 hours or up to overnight.

**2.** In the bowl of a stand mixer fitted with the whisk attachment, beat cold cream, vanilla, and salt at medium-high speed until stiff peaks form, 2 to

**3.** 3 minutes. Using a rubber spatula, gently fold whipped cream into pudding mixture in three additions until well combined and no streaks remain.

**4.** In bottom of a 13x9-inch baking dish, spread one-fourth of pudding mixture. Arrange half of banana slices on top. Spread one-fourth of pudding mixture onto banana slices. Top with half of vanilla wafers. Repeat layers once. Top with Whipped Cream. Loosely cover and refrigerate for at least 1 hour or up to 4 hours. Just before serving, garnish with banana slices and crushed vanilla wafers, if desired.

## FOR WHIPPED CREAM

**1.** In the bowl of stand mixer fitted with the whisk attachment, beat all ingredients at medium-high speed until stiff peaks form. Use immediately.

# CHOCOLATE CHIP & PEANUT BRITTLE COOKIE BARS

**MAKES 1 (13X9-INCH) PAN**

*Chunks of peanut brittle add a welcome crunch to these chocolate chip cookie bars. We used store-bought, but it's all the better if you have homemade brittle on hand!*

- **1 cup unsalted butter, softened**
- **1 cup granulated sugar**
- **1 cup firmly packed light brown sugar**
- **2 large eggs, room temperature**
- **1 tablespoon vanilla extract**
- **2¼ cups all-purpose flour**
- **1 teaspoon baking soda**
- **¾ teaspoon kosher salt**
- **2¼ cups milk chocolate chips, divided**
- **½ cup (¼- to ½-inch) broken peanut brittle pieces**

**1.** Preheat oven to 350°. Line a 13x9-inch baking pan with parchment paper, letting excess extend over sides of pan.

**2.** In a large bowl, beat butter and sugars with a mixer at medium speed until fluffy, 3 to 4 minutes, stopping to scrape sides of bowl. Add eggs, one at a time, beating well after each addition. Beat in vanilla.

**3.** In a medium bowl, whisk together flour, baking soda, and salt. With mixer on low speed, gradually add flour mixture to butter mixture, beating just until combined. Beat in 2 cups chocolate chips. Press dough into bottom of prepared pan.

**4.** Bake until a wooden pick inserted in center comes out with a few moist crumbs, 30 to 35 minutes, loosely covering with foil after 20 minutes of baking to prevent excess browning. Immediately sprinkle with remaining ¼ cup chocolate chips. Let cool completely in pan.

**5.** Using excess parchment as handles, remove from pan, and cut into bars. Sprinkle with peanut brittle just before serving.

# MOONPIE ICE CREAM CAKE

**MAKES ABOUT 6 SERVINGS**

*Created to satisfy a Kentucky coal miner's desire for a "snack as big as the moon," MoonPie's layers of graham cookie, marshmallow, and chocolate are still a Southern favorite 100 years later.*

- **1 (1½-quart) container chocolate chip ice cream, softened**
- **2 double-decker chocolate MoonPies, cut into 1-inch pieces**
- **2 cups frozen whipped topping, thawed**
- **Garnish: chopped chocolate MoonPies**

**1.** Line a 9x5-inch loaf pan with parchment paper or plastic wrap, letting excess extend over sides of pan.
**2.** Spread one-third of ice cream in bottom of prepared pan; sprinkle with half of chopped MoonPies. Repeat layers once. Spread remaining ice cream on top of loaf. Cover and freeze until firm.
**3.** Uncover; place a chilled plate over loaf, and invert loaf. Gently remove parchment or plastic wrap. Spread whipped topping on top of loaf. Garnish with chopped MoonPies, if desired. Serve immediately, or freeze until ready to serve.

# BROWNED BUTTER-SAGE APPLE CRISP

**MAKES 6 TO 8 SERVINGS**

*Rich browned butter and warm, aromatic sage transform this comforting, beloved dessert. Serve with a scoop of vanilla ice cream for a proper indulgence.*

**14 tablespoons unsalted butter, cubed**
**25 fresh sage leaves**
**1 cup all-purpose flour**
**⅔ cup quick-cooking oats**
**¾ cup firmly packed light brown sugar, divided**
**½ teaspoon kosher salt, divided**
**¼ teaspoon apple pie spice**
**6½ cups unpeeled (½-inch-thick) sliced Honeycrisp apples**
**2½ tablespoons cornstarch**
**1 tablespoon fresh lemon juice**
**Garnish: confectioners' sugar**

**1.** Preheat oven to 350°F (180°C).
**2.** In a 10-inch enamel-coated cast-iron skillet, melt butter over medium heat. Add sage; cook, stirring frequently, until butter turns a medium-brown color and has a nutty aroma, 7 to 12 minutes. Transfer to a medium bowl; let cool for 10 minutes. Remove sage using a slotted spoon; discard.
**3.** In a large bowl, whisk together flour, oats, ½ cup (110 grams) brown sugar, ¼ teaspoon salt, and apple pie spice. Add ½ cup (100 grams) browned butter, stirring just until combined.
**4.** Return remaining browned butter to skillet; add apples, cornstarch, lemon juice, remaining ¼ cup (55 grams) brown sugar, and remaining ¼ teaspoon salt, tossing to combine. Top apple mixture with oats mixture.
**5.** Bake until crisp is golden brown and filling is bubbly, 30 to 35 minutes. Let stand for 15 minutes before serving. Garnish with confectioners' sugar, if desired.

# PUMPKIN-PECAN PIE

**MAKES 1 (10-INCH) PIE**

*Two classic Thanksgiving pies come together to create one downright delicious dessert.*

- **1 (14.1-ounce) package refrigerated piecrusts**
- **1 (15-ounce) can pumpkin**
- **5 large eggs, divided**
- **¾ cup plus 2 tablespoons granulated sugar, divided**
- **⅓ cup firmly packed light brown sugar**
- **7 tablespoons unsalted butter, melted and divided**
- **¼ teaspoon ground cinnamon**
- **¼ teaspoon ground nutmeg**
- **1 cup light corn syrup**
- **1 tablespoon vanilla extract**
- **2 cups chopped pecans**

**1.** Preheat oven to 425°. Spray a 10-inch cast-iron skillet with cooking spray.
**2.** On a lightly floured surface, unroll piecrusts, and stack together; roll to a 14-inch circle. Press crust into bottom and up sides of prepared skillet. Fold edges of crust under, and crimp as desired. Line crust with parchment paper, letting excess parchment extend over sides; fill with pie weights.
**3.** Bake for 5 minutes. Let cool for 10 minutes; remove pie weights and parchment. Reduce oven temperature to 350°.
**4.** In a large bowl, whisk together pumpkin, 2 eggs, 2 tablespoons granulated sugar, brown sugar, 5 tablespoons melted butter, cinnamon, and nutmeg until smooth. Pour into prepared crust.
**5.** In same bowl, whisk together corn syrup, vanilla, remaining 3 eggs, remaining ¾ cup granulated sugar, and remaining 2 tablespoons melted butter until smooth. Stir in pecans. Gently pour mixture onto pumpkin layer.
**6.** Bake until center of pie is set, 50 minutes to 1 hour, covering edges of crust with foil to prevent excess browning, if needed. Let cool completely on a wire rack. Store pie in an airtight container for up to 3 days.

# FIG AND VANILLA BEAN UPSIDE-DOWN CORNMEAL CAKE

MAKES 1 (9-INCH) CAKE

*A toothsome, crunchy cornmeal cake and velvety caramelized fig bottom layer combine to create a dessert that triumphs in both texture and taste.*

- **¾ cup unsalted butter, softened and divided**
- **½ cup firmly packed light brown sugar**
- **12 fresh figs, sliced ¼ inch thick**
- **¾ cup granulated sugar**
- **3 large eggs**
- **1 cup fine yellow cornmeal**
- **⅔ cup all-purpose flour**
- **1½ teaspoons baking powder**
- **¾ teaspoon kosher salt**
- **¾ cup whole buttermilk**
- **2 teaspoons vanilla bean paste**

**1.** Preheat oven to 350°F (180°C). Line bottom of a 9-inch round cake pan with parchment paper; grease pan and parchment.

**2.** In a small saucepan, melt ¼ cup (57 grams) butter over low heat; stir in brown sugar. Pour into prepared pan. Arrange figs slightly overlapping on top of brown sugar mixture. Set aside.

**3.** In the bowl of a stand mixer fitted with the paddle attachment, beat granulated sugar and remaining ½ cup (113 grams) butter at medium speed until fluffy, 3 to 4 minutes, stopping to scrape sides of bowl. Add eggs, one at a time, beating well after each addition.

**4.** In a medium bowl, whisk together cornmeal, flour, baking powder, and salt. In a small bowl, whisk together buttermilk and vanilla bean paste. With mixer on low speed, gradually add cornmeal mixture to butter mixture alternately with buttermilk mixture, beginning and ending with flour mixture, beating just until combined after each addition. Pour batter over figs.

**5.** Bake until a wooden pick inserted in center comes out clean, 55 minutes to 1 hour. Let cool in pan for 15 minutes. Run a knife around edges of cake. Turn out onto a serving plate. Serve warm.

# BOURBON-WALNUT BROWN SUGAR CAKE

MAKES ABOUT 12 SERVINGS

*There's nothing like bourbon to warm the soul, which is why we let the aromatic spirit star in this grown-up version of your favorite brown sugar cake.*

**CAKE**

- **1 cup unsalted butter, softened**
- **1½ cups firmly packed dark brown sugar**
- **4 large eggs**
- **1 teaspoon vanilla bean paste**
- **3 cups cake flour**
- **2 teaspoons baking powder**
- **1 teaspoon ground cinnamon**
- **½ teaspoon baking soda**
- **½ teaspoon kosher salt**
- **1 cup whole milk**
- **½ cup bourbon**
- **¾ cup chopped walnuts**

**BUTTERCREAM**

- **1 cup unsalted butter, softened**
- **2 cups confectioners' sugar**
- **2 teaspoons heavy whipping cream**
- **2 teaspoons vanilla bean paste**
- **⅛ teaspoon kosher salt**
- **8 ounces mascarpone cheese**

**Garnish: chopped walnuts**

**FOR CAKE**

**1.** Preheat oven to 325°F. Spray a 13x9-inch baking pan with cooking spray. Line pan with parchment paper, letting excess extend over sides of pan; spray pan again.

**2.** In the bowl of a stand mixer fitted with the paddle attachment, beat butter and brown sugar at medium speed until fluffy, 3 to 4 minutes, stopping to scrape sides of bowl. Add eggs, one at a time, beating well after each addition. Beat in vanilla bean paste.

**3.** In a medium bowl, whisk together flour, baking powder, cinnamon, baking soda, and salt. In a small bowl, whisk together milk and bourbon. With mixer on low speed, gradually add flour mixture to butter mixture alternately with milk mixture, beginning and ending with flour mixture, beating just until combined after each addition. Fold in walnuts. Pour batter into prepared pan, smoothing top with an offset spatula.

**4.** Bake until a wooden pick inserted in center comes out clean, 35 to 40 minutes. Let cool completely in pan. Using excess parchment as handles, remove from pan. Spread Mascarpone Buttercream onto cooled cake. Garnish with walnuts, if desired.

**FOR BUTTERCREAM**

**1.** In the bowl of a stand mixer fitted with the paddle attachment, beat butter at medium speed until creamy. Increase mixer speed to medium-high. Gradually add confectioners' sugar, beating until fluffy, 3 to 4 minutes. Add cream, vanilla bean paste, and salt; beat until combined. Fold in mascarpone cheese by hand, and stir until combined. (Be careful not to overmix mascarpone. It will begin to separate and start to weep.) Use immediately.

# KITCHEN SINK COOKIE

**MAKES 6 TO 8 SERVINGS**

*The "less is more" mentality simply doesn't apply to this epic cookie. Pretzels, potato chips, caramel, and chocolate—this sweet treat has all the textures and flavors you could ever want.*

- **1 cup unsalted butter, softened**
- **1 cup packed light brown sugar**
- **½ cup granulated sugar**
- **2 large eggs**
- **2 teaspoons vanilla extract**
- **1¼ cups all-purpose flour**
- **2 cups old-fashioned oats**
- **1 teaspoon baking soda**
- **½ teaspoon baking powder**
- **1½ teaspoons kosher salt**
- **1 cup mini candy-coated chocolate pieces, divided**
- **½ cup caramel bits**
- **1 cup lightly crushed kettle-cooked potato chips, divided**
- **1 cup broken mini twist pretzels, divided**
- **¾ cup dark chocolate chunks**

**1.** Preheat oven to 350°. Spray a 10-inch square enameled cast-iron pan with baking spray with flour.

**2.** In the bowl of a stand mixer fitted with the paddle attachment, beat butter and sugars at medium speed until fluffy, 3 to 4 minutes, stopping to scrape sides of bowl. Reduce mixer speed to medium-low. Add eggs, one at a time, beating well after each addition. Beat in vanilla.

**3.** In a medium bowl, whisk together flour, oats, baking soda, baking powder, and salt. Reduce mixer speed to low. Gradually add flour mixture to butter mixture, beating just until combined (do not overmix). Gently stir in ¾ cup candy-coated chocolate pieces, caramel bits, ¾ cup potato chips, ¾ cup pretzels, and chocolate chunks. Press batter into prepared pan. Sprinkle remaining ¼ cup mini candy-coated chocolate pieces, ¼ cup pretzels, and ¼ cup potato chips over top.

**4.** Bake until edges are browned and center is set but soft, 30 to 35 minutes, or to desired degree of doneness, covering after 10 minutes to prevent overbrowning, if needed. Let cool on a wire rack. Serve warm or at room temperature.

# CHOCOLATE ESPRESSO MARTINI TRIFLES

MAKES 4 TO 6 SERVINGS

*Traditionally layers of cake, custard, and fruit, the trifle gets a modern makeover. Whether serving in individual glasses or in one big dish, everyone will love this decadent dessert.*

**TRIFLES**
- **¾ cup hot strong-brewed coffee**
- **6 ounces bittersweet chocolate, chopped**
- **2½ cups heavy whipping cream, divided**
- **½ cup confectioners' sugar, divided**
- **1 cup mascarpone cheese**
- **¼ cup coffee liqueur**
- **Garnish: chopped chocolate-covered coffee beans, cocoa powder**

**FUDGE BROWNIES**
- **½ cup all-purpose flour**
- **½ cup unsweetened cocoa powder**
- **½ teaspoon kosher salt**
- **1 cup firmly packed light brown sugar**
- **½ cup unsalted butter, melted and cooled slightly**
- **2 large eggs**
- **1½ teaspoons vanilla extract**

## FOR TRIFLES

**1.** In a large bowl, whisk together hot coffee and chocolate until chocolate is melted and mixture is smooth. Let cool completely.

**2.** In the bowl of a stand mixer fitted with the whisk attachment, beat 1½ cups cream and ¼ cup confectioners' sugar at medium-high speed until stiff peaks form, 2 to 3 minutes. Fold whipped cream mixture into coffee mixture in three additions until just combined. Cover and refrigerate until set, about 2 hours.

**3.** Clean bowl of stand mixer and whisk attachment. Using the whisk attachment, beat remaining 1 cup cream and remaining ¼ cup confectioners' sugar at medium-high speed until stiff peaks form, 2 to 3 minutes.

**4.** In another large bowl, stir together mascarpone and liqueur until smooth. Fold whipped cream mixture into liqueur mixture in two additions until just combined.

**5.** Layer chocolate-coffee mousse and Fudge Brownies in desired glasses. Top with mascarpone whipped cream. Using an offset spatula, smooth top so it's level with the glass. Garnish with coffee beans and cocoa, if desired.

## FOR FUDGE BROWNIES

**1.** Preheat oven to 350°. Lightly spray an 8-inch square baking dish with baking spray with flour.

**2.** In a medium bowl, whisk together flour, cocoa, and salt.

**3.** In a large bowl, whisk together brown sugar and melted butter until well combined. Add eggs and vanilla, whisking until well combined and smooth. Gradually add flour mixture, stirring until just combined. Spoon into prepared pan, spreading to edges of pan.

**4.** Bake until set, 20 to 25 minutes. Let cool for 25 to 30 minutes before cutting as desired.

# VANILLA BEAN BUTTERMILK CAKE

MAKES 1 (10-INCH) CAKE

*The vanilla bean seeds in this simple frosting give this cake an extra punch of vanilla flavor.*

**CAKE**

- **¾ cup unsalted butter, softened**
- **1½ cups plus 1 tablespoon sugar, divided**
- **3 large eggs**
- **2 teaspoons vanilla extract**
- **2 cups all-purpose flour**
- **1¾ teaspoons baking powder**
- **½ teaspoon kosher salt**
- **1 cup whole buttermilk**
- **1½ cups fresh raspberries**

**FROSTING**

- **1 cup unsalted butter, softened**
- **3 ounces cream cheese, softened**
- **1 vanilla bean, split lengthwise, seeds scraped and reserved**
- **2½ cups confectioners' sugar**
- **1 tablespoon whole buttermilk**

## FOR CAKE

**1.** Preheat oven to 350°. Spray a 10-inch cast-iron skillet with cooking spray.

**2.** In a large bowl, beat butter and 1½ cups sugar with a mixer at medium speed until fluffy, 3 to 4 minutes, stopping to scrape sides of bowl. Add eggs, one at a time, beating well after each addition. Stir in vanilla.

**3.** In a medium bowl, whisk together flour, baking powder, and salt. With mixer on low speed, gradually add flour mixture to butter mixture alternately with buttermilk, beginning and ending with flour mixture, beating just until combined after each addition. Spread batter in prepared skillet.

**4.** Bake until a wooden pick inserted in center comes out clean, 35 to 40 minutes, loosely covering with foil to prevent excess browning, if necessary. Let cool completely in pan .

**5.** In a small bowl, toss together raspberries and remaining 1 tablespoon sugar. Let stand until raspberries are glossy, about 5 minutes. Spread Frosting on top of cake. Garnish with raspberries, if desired.

## FOR FROSTING

**1.** In a large bowl, beat butter, cream cheese, and reserved vanilla bean seeds with a mixer at medium speed until creamy. Add confectioners' sugar, beating until combined. Stir in buttermilk until a spreadable consistency is reached.

*index*

## BREADS



## DESSERTS



## MAINS—BEEF & PORK



## MAINS—POULTRY



## MAINS—SEAFOOD & VEGETARIAN

## PASTAS



## SIDES



## SOUPS & SALAD